THE ALLYN AND BACON GUIDE TO PEER TUTORING

Paula Gillespie
Marquette University

Neal Lerner
Massachusetts College of Pharmacy & Health Sciences

Allyn and Bacon
Boston • London • Toronto • Sydney • Tokyo • Singapore

Vice President: Eben W. Ludlow
Editorial Assistant: Grace Trudo
Executive Marketing Manager: Lisa Kimball
Editorial Production Service: Chestnut Hill Enterprises, Inc.
Manufacturing Buyer: Suzanne Lareau
Cover Administrator: Jennifer Hart

Internet: www.abacon.com

Between the time web site information is gathered and published, some sites may
have closed. Also, the transcription of URLs can result in typographical errors. The
publisher would appreciate notification where these occur so that they may be
corrected in subsequent editions.

Library of Congress Cataloging-in-Publication Data

Gillespie, Paula.
   The Allyn and Bacon guide to peer tutoring / Paula Gillespie, Neal
Lerner.
     p. cm.
   Includes bibliographical references (p.) and index.
   ISBN 0-205-29766-8
   1. Peer-group tutoring of students. 2. Tutors and tutoring.
3. Writing centers. I. Lerner, Neal. II. Title. III. Title:
Guide to peer tutoring.
LB1031.5.G55 2000
371.39'4—dc21   99-35773
                                                      CIP

Printed in the United States of America
10 9 8 7 6 5 4 3 2 1   04 03 02 01 00 99

CONTENTS

PREFACE

Like many writing projects, *The Allyn and Bacon Guide to Peer Tutoring* grew out of conversations that we've had over the years, whether that talk has been through telephone lines, in front of computer screens, or face-to-face. When the subject of those conversations was tutor training, we agreed that our contribution to the field would be marked by the presence of tutors through reflective papers, tutoring journals, or session transcripts. It seems unfortunately trite to say that we've learned amazing amounts from those tutors with whom we've worked or directly trained, as well as from the many, many writers we've had the good fortune to meet in writing center work. But it's true—those tutors and writers have been among our greatest teachers, and we knew that a tutor-training text should be steeped in their accounts.

We also believe that the structure of our text should mirror the structure of tutor training, starting with overviews of the writing and tutoring process (Chapters 2 and 3); followed by some self-examination of what one brings to tutoring (Chapter 4); and then concrete instruction in observing (Chapter 5); trying out the roles of tutor, writer, and observer (Chapter 6); practicing with students' essays (Chapter 7); and then making sense of those first tutoring experiences (Chapter 8). We also felt that we should support our readers' study of tutoring with more depth on "specialized" topics: reading in the writing center Chapter 9), working with non-native English speakers (Chapter 10), conducting writing center research through discourse analysis (Chapter 11), tutoring on-line (Chapter 12), and viewing tutoring through the lens of writing center ethics (Chapter 13). Finally, we also felt that any guide would need to anticipate common scenarios and offer some general advice on how to deal with those potential challenges (Chapter 14).

Although there's certainly a sequence to these chapters, we also intend any single chapter to stand alone and we want to allow our readers to pick and choose depending upon their particular needs. Along those lines, rather than include readings that might reflect *our* particular needs, we've instead included a list of suggested readings, as well as a list of works cited.

These are exciting times for us in the writing center field. A thriving national organization and a publishing house, two journals dedicated to our scholarship, a growing number of regional organizations, and a host of new publications—all are evidence of the increasing recognition of the power of the one-to-one teaching of writing. As writing centers grow at all instructional levels, so does the need to have skilled, prepared tutors. We hope that this guide can contribute to that end.

ACKNOWLEDGMENTS

We both want to thank Eben Ludlow of Allyn and Bacon for his never-wavering support of this project, even in its earliest, most sketchy form. Tania Sanchez of Allyn and Bacon also provided her able assistance. In addition, we're indebted to the reviewers of our original proposal for this book and the reviewers of early drafts—Albert C. DeCiccio, Merrimack College/Wheelock College; Muriel Harris, Purdue University; James C. McDonald, University of Southwestern Louisiana; Jon Olson, The Pennsylvania State University; and Bruce Pegg, Colgate University. Their thoughtful and helpful comments allowed us to reimagine just what this book could be and for whom. We'd also like to thank the many contributors to the Internet listserv WCenter over the last several years. Many of our ideas for tutor training were gleaned and refined from that discussion list, and it continues to be a vital source of support, encouragement, and collegiality. Bobbie Silk, Jon Olson, Katie Fischer, and Stephen Newmann have been our vital support system for many years now; this book would not have been possible without them.

Neal would like to thank Nicole Hein for her helpful feedback, Tania Baker for her steadfast support, and Hannah Baker-Lerner for her sweet presence.

Paula would like to thank Michael and Ann Gillespie, Karen Dhanens, and Leigh and Torrey Pike for their encouragement and support. Many thanks to all of the tutors in the Norman H. Ott Memorial Writing Center and students in English 192 for their excellent ideas and help. Special thanks to Thomas Wicker, Virginia Chappell, Krista Ratcliffe, John McCabe, and Tim Machan at Marquette and to Alice Gillam for inspiration; for good ideas and friendship, Kathleen Yancey, Laura Julier, Carl Glover, Byron Stay, Lady Falls Brown, Muriel Harris, Joyce Steward, and Joan Mullin. Thanks to Pat Reihle and Craig Woytal for all their good-natured clerical help. Deepest gratitude to the family of Norman H. Ott for its generous support of the Writing Center.

ABOUT THE AUTHORS

In the chapters that follow, we offer advice to deal with the complexities of tutoring. However, we don't want to obscure the joy that writing center work will bring you. Instead, we want to open this textbook by giving you a sense of our experience and of the joy that we have found in writing center work. We want you to know how we came to this point as writing center directors and textbook writers before we retreat back into third-person stances.

First, Paula:

I'd tutored in what used to be called the Writing Lab at the University of Wisconsin, Madison when I was a graduate student back in the 70s, and I'd enjoyed it. We went far beyond the drill-and-kill centers you sometimes read about in the literature of that era because the director, Joyce Steward, was ahead of her time, really breaking ground for writing centers. But when I left Madison, my writing center work ended for a few years.

I taught part-time for a while at Marquette, had a baby, and finished up my exams and courses for my doctorate. The Marquette writing center hummed along just down the hall from me, and I referred my students there as I taught sections of first-year comp and sophomore literature.

But then things changed at Marquette. They put into place an innovative writing program that changed the focus from classical rhetoric and "the modes of discourse" to the process of writing. This program was similar to the one I'd been trained in at Madison when I taught developmental writers there, so when a new full-time job opened, I applied for it and got it. My duties eventually included directing the writing center.

I had never envisioned myself as a writing center director before, but I began reading everything I could get my hands on, and I was sent to spend a few days in New York City with Lil Brannon, who directed the writing center at NYU. A few years earlier, Lil had started up a writing center in a closet—literally in a closet—because she believed so strongly in collaborative learning and in the power of tutoring. She established and edited the Writing Center Journal, *and she had a busy and exciting writing center. She made me feel optimistic not only about directing a center but about the goals and possibilities of tutoring.*

I began tutoring alongside the new graduate student tutors rather than just directing the center, and I found that our common ground made me a better director for being part of the tutoring. But it was more than that: I found that I really, really enjoyed tutoring.

My favorite tutoring experiences came when writers would stay with me through their four years of college. I remember Jane, an older student who struggled to pass her writing courses at first, but who grew in her mastery of writing as the years and courses came and went. She'd never been taught to write essays or to document sources, and she struggled to make her verbs agree with the subjects so that she met the requirements of academic discourse. We spent a lot of time looking at her verbs, but after some time she was finding them herself and fixing them on her own. And with her leaps-and-bounds improvements in grammar and correctness came an increasingly sophisticated ability to read and interpret texts. I don't know what caused what, but I know that her self-respect grew along with her writing ability.

And I remember Tahseena, who came to this country from Pakistan without having studied English, and who also struggled, but wanted to be a philosophy major because a course had made her catch fire. My favorite meeting with her took place outdoors rather than in the writing center where we'd worked together. One day she passed me on campus, waving a philosophy paper in the air. "I got an AB on it! And I did it all by myself!" She didn't need me any more; that's a sad but delicious experience.

But it isn't only those long-term relationships we develop with writers that make me love tutoring. It's the excitement in a session of helping a writer with an ok draft turn it into a really dynamic idea that she's eager to revise. And it's the fun of helping a writer brainstorm to find just the right topic. And it isn't just the sessions that go well, but the challenge of those sessions that don't go well that I love. At our staff meetings, we put our heads together and solve tutoring problems, or try to. And I love talking about tutoring. I've enjoyed working on this book with Neal; I've learned a lot about tutoring not just from the writing we've done together, but also from the tutors, graduate and undergraduate, that I work with. Most of the writing that I'm required to do is hard work, just as it is for the writers I tutor, but this was fun. Revising it has been fun, too, because I keep learning.

Next, Neal's story:

My teaching career started with writing center work. After an uneven career as an undergraduate English major and after several years of working in the computer industry, I enrolled in a graduate English/Creative Writing program at San Jose State University, pursuing my master's degree. My short-term goal was to write fiction and live off student loans (I don't think I had any long-term goals). However, I soon found that I needed additional work to pay my rent and buy the occasional sandwich. In the fall of the first year, I applied to work in the SJSU Writing Center. I hadn't had any experience as a writing teacher (and thus couldn't secure a coveted teaching assistant position), but I had taken a seminar course in my first semester on "Practical Approaches to Composition." In that course, I became intrigued by the study of the writing process and the challenge of teaching others to write. The application process for the SJSU Writing Center involved responding to a student's text and completing a short-answer grammar exam. I did fine with the text response but bombed the exam (despite having written a great deal since my undergraduate days, at that time I couldn't tell you the difference between a noun modifier and burnt toast). For some reason, the director of the writing center saw some potential and agreed to hire me, provided that at the same time I would enroll in a class on English grammar and usage.

I loved tutoring from the very first. I was working primarily with students in basic writing courses or ones who had been in a non-college-level track in high school and found themselves unprepared for college-level work. Many of the students were of Asian or Latino descent, anxious to claim their share of the "American Dream," and frustrated over how their language proficiency was holding them back. But they were also very grateful to be getting the attention and instruction that the Writing Center could provide. As far as the grammar class went, I even found that work to be enjoyable after a while, once I had broken the "secret code" of grammar terminology.

After getting my MA and then a high-school teaching credential, I worked as an adjunct English teacher at a variety of places across the country. But one-to-one instruction, whether in a writing center or privately, was a constant thread. By the time I found myself in Boston, in a doctorate of Education program at Boston University, writing center work provided several important directions. One was to give me a chance to return to the teaching of writing at the Boston University Writing Center after several semesters of teaching foundations of education. The other was to give me a dissertation topic when I embarked upon a two-year study of the tutors and writers who used one particular writing center. I was fascinated (and still am) by the experiences and expectations that tutors and writers bring to their sessions, and how those notions translate into the language each participant uses.

Near the end of my program, I also started tutoring at the Massachusetts Institute of Technology Writing Center, working with a steady stream of technically-minded undergraduates and graduate students, all trying to make meaning of and seeking help in that pursuit.

Three years ago, I was hired to start a writing center at the Massachusetts College of Pharmacy and Health Sciences in Boston. Students at MCP/HS take required first-year composition and also have other courses and professional tasks with a strong writing component. Nearly 60 percent of the writers who have come to the MCP/HS Writing Center are ESL, and my consultants are a combination of peer tutors and "professional" staff who are MA-, MFA-, or PhD-level writing instructors. I still tutor in the Writing Center, as well as teach first-year composition. My one-to-one work always reminds me that it is often one-to-one that we can most successfully teach writing. I firmly believes in the words of Mina Shaugnessy, who wrote that "the teaching of writing must often begin with the experience of dialogue and end with the experience of a real audience." Writing center tutors are that "real audience" and engage student writers in that dialogue.

1

WHY WE TUTOR

This is a book about tutoring writing. You'll read about the techniques of tutoring, the theoretical and practical background that you'll need to be successful, and the specific issues that make writing center work both challenging and rewarding.

To introduce you to tutoring writing and to how we hope this book will help you, we want to start at the beginning. Why do we tutor? The answer to that question forms, for us, the foundation upon which our own lives as tutors and writing center directors are based, and informs each chapter of this book.

We'll first explore the question "Why tutor?" by turning to some voices that you'll hear again and again in this book—the trainees in the Marquette University peer tutoring course. Much that is offered here has been "tried out" on that willing and generous group, and we, as coauthors, have learned a great deal from their experiences. We think you, too, will find much familiarity with the stories they tell; but in particular, in this chapter, they will talk about what they expected tutoring to be like at the beginning of their course and where they believe those expectations came from. We believe that learning anything new starts with thinking about what you already know and then building upon that knowledge. As you read these responses, think about the experiences that you bring to tutoring writing. From Jessi:

> I remember when I was in fourth grade, I was singled out (I hate when teachers do that) to help a slow kid named Peter with his reading. We sat down during "quiet time" and I helped him go over the lesson we had learned earlier that day. Each day when we were done, the teacher

would give me a sticker, I assume as a reward, that I had to wear on the front of my Catholic school uniform. She never gave Peter a sticker.

Today I am still undecided as to why I was chosen to help Peter. Was it because I have always been good at matters pertaining to English? Did the teacher think Peter would benefit more from my help as a peer? Or was she just lazy and preferred to have "quiet time" to herself? I guess I don't expect a sticker at the end of each of my tutoring sessions these days. I do expect tutoring to be a fulfilling experience for both myself and my students/classmates. I hope to give them something they can walk away with and apply later on, whether it be on that paper or a future one. I hope I can take something I have learned and help them use that knowledge to become better writers.

From Paul:

In my high school, being a tutor meant being a really good speller and knowing MLA style. In fact I remember one of my sophomore year English teachers saying to class one day that with computers being able to spell check and grammar check, proof readers won't be necessary anymore. Now I took this little "gem" of knowledge to mean that tutors were going to be obsolete. Why go and get your writing checked when the computer does it for you? The answer came my freshman year when I went to the writing center. I don't remember my tutor's name. All I remember was he did not care one ounce about my spelling. He wanted to make sure that the paper "flowed." I was dumbfounded; I had no idea what he was talking about. In fact, I didn't even follow his suggestions because anything he said went against the Introduction-Three-Paragraph-Conclusion format I had learned in high school. Well, Dr. Miller gave me a D. I rewrote the paper with the suggestions that my tutor gave me. I got a B.

I learned (the hard way) that tutoring is more than just proof reading. Its about getting the person to realize that there is always more than one set way to go about writing a paper.

From Aesha:

For most of my career as a student, I basically wanted to please my teachers. I was concerned about getting a smiley face on my paper or having my teacher read my paper aloud as an example of what to do for an "A." Therefore, if there was something wrong with my writing that my teachers didn't like, I changed it, even if I liked it. Somehow, I equated an "A" in English from my fifth-grade teacher to mean that she liked me as a person. It wasn't until I came to college that these expectations changed. My English 001 professor, Dr. Gervasi, challenged me to examine my thought processes. If my paper was not "A" material on the first draft, it did not necessarily mean that I was somehow not good enough. Dr. Gervasi showed me this by not being so excited about my hurried grammatical changes (my grade reflected this) as he was about the way I strengthened my support of opinions or even when I changed my mind.

In other words, I don't want the tutee to think that I am somehow judging his/her personality when we are in a session. I want it to be clear that my suggestions, etc. are not the last word, but that he/she must decide what works.

From Megan:

I was a junior in high school, and never having struggled with a class, I was forced by my parental units to seek out a tutor in order to find success in physics. As I knew physics would not play a very important part in my future, I needed not to "understand" but rather to pull out of the class having created the idea that I was physics-minded. Mr. Martinson came highly recommended by a number of my friends. Soon, I found out why. We met at the library for our one-hour session. I would hand him my book and my assignment, and he would proceed to complete each problem, showing his work clearly, and usually with a diagram. I would then take the work home, having been "tutored," and I would copy it, memorize it, and give it to any of my friends who also were struggling. I passed physics, and well too, but in retrospect I know that I have little idea what speed two tennis balls shot from opposite sides of the room would have to be thrown in order for them to meet exactly in the middle of the room.

So this being my experience when I became a peer tutor my senior year, I knew what not to do. Don't do their work. Try to simplify the problem. Have the other person explain what they think they are doing wrong. These were the steps I would take.

As a tutor in the writing center, I can see how easy it would be to get "Mr. Martinson Syndrome": to take the dreaded red pen to a paper and edit and rewrite. But I know this is highly ineffective. So to sum it all up: I think my preconceptions about tutoring are only that I am not here to do the work but to help someone else be proud of the work that they have done without feeling that unnecessary struggle is required.

From Adele:

When I was in high school, I started my freshman year out in "honors" English. After that first year, I was asked to move down to regular English because good ol' Mrs. Johnson thought I could "handle" it better.

That ruined most of my aspirations for writing. I accepted C's because I figured I just wasn't a good writer. God must have given me some other talent, and I tried to find it.

It wasn't until sophomore year of college that I found writing again. Thanks to Dr. McBride's English Lit class, I figured out how to write for myself. Prior to this, I never saw the point in tutoring because I always viewed it as a bashing session by "Mrs. Johnson." And Lord knows we all get defensive when our work is torn to shreds by some dominant little know-it-all. So, anyway, I went to talk to McBride about my first analytical paper, expecting him to scrape up all the little lost pieces. I was desperate. But I was totally thrown off by our meeting. The head of the department wanted to know what I thought; HE was the expert! But that session taught me that the writer is the expert. It was MY damn paper, and I had to learn how to write it.

From Sara:

Most of my experiences with tutoring in high school left a bad taste in my mouth. Because I was a good student and a fairly good writer for a high school student, my teachers would often ask me to work with other students who were struggling. Or my friends, who knew that I got good grades, would come to me with questions about homework assignments. A lot of my study halls would get eaten up by answering questions about subjects from chemistry to English. I enjoyed helping people and didn't mind the time I spent with them, but many times I would end up feeling used. I would get sick of working on assignments with people who just wanted to get to the bottom line, but who didn't care about the whole process behind getting there. Looking back on those experiences after our discussions and readings, I see now that I wanted to be a "minimalist" tutor who caused others to think about their writing or other assignments, but I didn't know how to do that.

Since high school, I have worked at the Educational Opportunity Program over in Marquette Hall as a tutor for the Upward Bound program. My experiences there have been a lot better than those in high school. I haven't ever tutored writing, but I learned by working there that the student learns best when he or she does the work. I, as a tutor, am not there to solve their every problem with the assignment, but to help them think through how they can solve those problems on their own. In some ways, I think the goal of a tutor should be to make yourself obsolete. I hope that all of the students I worked with at EOP learned to problem solve on their own. Like Paula said in class—it's okay that the freshmen didn't come back to the writing center after their first time, so long as they were equipped the first time with the tools to successfully critique their own writing.

As you read these accounts, you might have noticed several common themes. Almost all had their expectations of tutoring formed by being put in a "teacherly" position or by being tutored themselves. And almost all of these writers didn't like the position of being a "know-it-all"; instead, they have learned that tutoring involves helping someone become a better writer, not handing out vocabulary words or cleaning up someone else's paper (and we'll talk much more about the differences between tutoring and editing in Chapter 3). As Sara wrote, "I, as a tutor, am not there to solve [writers'] every problem with the assignment, but to help them think through how they can solve those problems on their own." So, how do you do that?

CONTRASTING CONCEPTS

One other theme from the tutor stories is that many concepts that surround tutoring writing seem to be in opposition—tutor/editor, novice/expert, process/product, control/flexibility, tutor/teacher. These contrasts frame many of the minute-by-minute decisions we make as tutors. In this book we will expand on each of these contrasts, showing how experienced tutors don't simply reject one concept in favor of its opposite, but instead adjust their actions by being sensitive to a writer's needs and the context for any individual tutoring session. In other words, each of these contrasts exists as ends of a continuum, and any place on that scale contains qualities of both extremes. As an analogy, imagine a color scale with blue on one end and yellow on the other. The exact middle of that scale is green—a fifty-fifty blending of blue and yellow—but as you get closer to the blue end, that green becomes bluer and bluer, and when you get closer to the yellow end, that green begins to pale. In this text we'll often refer to concepts that aren't either/or choices (for example, we won't claim that writing center work is *either* challenging *or* rewarding—it's both!), but instead we'll invoke these contrasts to attest to the complexity of the work you are about to enter. You'll often find yourself closer to one end of the continuum than the other, sometimes in the middle, sometimes at several places over the course of any given session. If this technique sounds active and responsive, well, those are two qualities that experienced tutors often display.

One additional contrast is the prescriptive/descriptive continuum. In this book, we don't want necessarily to *prescribe* what we think an effective tutor should do; after all, there's no way we can anticipate every situation you'll find yourself in, nor do we think that the best way for you to learn is for us to *tell* you what you should be doing. Instead, we'll mainly *describe*, allowing new and experienced tutors to do much of the talking, whether that's in the form of first-person accounts, essays, or transcripts from actual sessions. Although some of the advice we give might come off as more "telling" than "showing," our ultimate goal for you is to use this book in order to become a more strategic tutor, to have a variety of resources you can call upon to help you succeed in any tutoring situation, and to pose questions so that you can learn from your experiences. We think we know what has worked for us as tutors, and we'll share that advice (as will many peer tutors you'll hear from), but you'll have to adapt that advice to your contexts, your individual style, and your needs. In jazz improvisation, learning a new sequence often starts with copying someone else's "spontaneous" riff; after a while, you make that riff your own, adding shading, tone, or sounds that are uniquely you. So it goes with tutoring writing. We hope our book can contribute to that development.

THE WRITING CENTER AND THE WRITING PROCESS

In the next chapter we'll delve more deeply into the writing process and what it means for you both personally and as a tutor. First, however, we want you to consider both the role of the writing center in the ways that writers approach an assignment and how you as a tutor will represent the writing center. The following are two undergraduate writers' descriptions of their writing processes:

Dyana, a sophomore English major:

> Traditionally when I hear about a paper usually it's two weeks in advance till the due date, and I usually put it off for about a day or two, and then I go and do some research regardless of what the paper is. I always do library research just to get a better feel for what I'm doing. And then I jot down some ideas and then usually walk away from it for about a day. And then a lot of times I'll go to the writing center without anything, without having anything really except notes written and just say, "Okay this is what I need to do," because I really need to talk through my ideas to actually develop them. I can sit there and think about them, but they won't come into words unless I talk through them. And so I kind of just go there a lot of times to bounce things off of [my tutor], and she gives me a lot of insight, too. But then I usually write like two, sometimes if I'm feeling very ambitious, three drafts. That's about my whole process.

Yu, a School of Management freshman:

> I will first read the [assignment]. And then after that I try to think about
> what I can do without reading [the assigned text]. And then I start read-
> ing [the assigned text] for the first time, without taking notes. And after
> that I just throw the [readings] away for awhile. And I go back and then
> take notes like I'm marking what's important. And I try to keep thinking
> [about] what I should write between the time that I decided to write and
> the time I finish my reading. Before I start writing I would normally read
> an editorial in the newspaper where I will just pick it up and read it and
> then I will do my writing for the first time. I think [an] editorial provides
> background, and also it's just weird that I think it gets me started.

You might see familiarities in these descriptions, as well as distinct differences from the writing processes you use. Such is the idiosyncratic nature of
writing.

From Dyana's description above, you can see that some writers know
well how the writing center can help. For others, particularly for writers who
are required to meet with you, it might not be so obvious. As a representative
of the writing center, you have a chance to work with writers to help them
understand just how helpful you can be. Ideally, writers will meet with you
several times over the course of their completing any writing task: when the
paper is first assigned so that together you can clarify the assignment and
brainstorm initial ideas; after the writer has done some drafting so that you
can discuss points of development or possible ways of structuring the ideas;
while the writer is revising so that you can guide him or her to focus on the
"higher-order" concerns and put aside editing/proofreading until the very
end; and in that very end so that you can help the writer become a more
detailed reader of his or her own work (and we'll share lots of strategies for
these roles throughout this book). Overall, you can help writers learn how
to learn, an idea that we'll discuss in the next two chapters.

We bring up this topic because it might happen that you see writers
whose understanding of the writing tutor's role is that of proofreader or
cleaner of texts—more contrasts that complicate our work. Just as less-
experienced writers exhibit less-developed strategies when they write, less-
experienced writers do not fully appreciate the collaborative nature of
writing and how important a writing tutor can be at any point in the process. Once again, you have an opportunity not only to increase a writers'
strategic repertoire, but to stress the role the writing center can play. Muriel
Harris has noted that "all writers need writing tutors," and this is the foundation upon which modern writing centers are based.

IT'S A MATTER OF TRUST

You might have noticed that we use the term "writer" to refer to those folks whom we work with in our writing centers. We've chosen this term with specific purpose. While "student," "tutee," "client," or "respondent" all are accurate descriptions to a degree, we truly believe that it's important for you to see the people you work with as writers, just as you are. Of course, writers are at various levels of accomplishment and experience, but all intend to find meaning in what they write and to share that meaning with others. We trust all writers' intentions.

Trust is essential to much of the writing and tutoring process; perhaps most important, writers need to trust themselves, whether to have the patience to wade through pages of a truly rough draft, the kind of writing they wouldn't dare show anyone else (as the early versions of this book were), or the trust writers need in order to know that they can turn that rough writing into polished prose. Writers also need to trust their readers (whether real or imagined). Readers will do what the writer asks, at least initially: Accept the premises of the argument if it's logical; follow the thread of a narrative if it's entertaining; picture the details of a description if it's well rendered. So many "ifs," it seems. Perhaps that's why the writing process is such a complicated act, one seemingly both social and individual, public and private at the same time. You might be writing away in your room, on a park bench, or in your backyard, feeling isolated or at least oblivious to the immediate world around you. Yet, at the same time, you're in a social world, one that involves you, your reader, and your content. Even if you're writing fiction, you're creating a social world; in many kinds of nonfiction you're recreating a world in order to render it faithfully to your reader.

Trust is no less important in the relationship between tutors and writers. It's one thing to know and to trust the ways that work best for you as a writer. It's an entirely different thing to consider the ways that the writing center tutor functions within students' writing processes. As a student and a successful writer, you have great insight to share. As a writing center tutor, you'll create an atmosphere of trust for the writers who seek your help. In that environment, you and the writers with whom you meet can accomplish truly important work.

It's also essential that you trust yourself—as a tutor and as a peer. You have the unique opportunity to accomplish work that most teachers cannot do: You're not going to give a grade to a writer's essay, you have great insight into what it means to be a student, and you'll have many things in common with many of the writers you meet. You need to trust these great advantages; the rapport that you can create with writers is one of your best assets as a tutor.

So why do we tutor? Well, what we have learned is that tutoring allows us to connect, whether it's with writers' ideas, with their struggle to make meaning, or simply with the simple fact of them as fellow human beings sitting beside us in the writing center.

We hope the chapters in this book help you gain an understanding of why you tutor, both now and by the time you are an old hand at helping student writers. You'll learn about the writing and the tutoring process, and spend more time thinking about the expectations you bring to tutoring. You'll also have concrete guidance in taking your first steps toward observing, participating in, and then analyzing your writing center sessions. Finally, we'll focus on specific kinds of challenges you'll encounter: writers with reading difficulties, ESL writers, and writers who present a variety of ethical and practical dilemmas.

Most important, we want to welcome you to an experience that can change your life if you allow it to, just as it has done for us. That's a grand promise, we know, but we don't make it lightly. We offer that promise as an invitation—to come explore the work of tutoring writing. We hope that this book can act as a trustworthy guide in that exploration.

2

THE WRITING PROCESS

You're considering becoming a writing tutor or are already tutoring because you've had some success as a writer yourself. That's no small feat. Writing is one of the most difficult—and most rewarding—things anyone can do. And perhaps your motives for tutoring are to pass on to others what it is you know how to do well. For someone who likes to write, the opportunity to talk with others about their writing and then get paid for it (or receive course credit) is quite a good deal. You'll find many others like you in the writing center field who love talking about language and writing and helping others use language in important ways.

Keep in mind that talking about writing is perhaps the most important thing you will do as a tutor, and contrast that talk with what's often seen as "teaching." Teaching any subject is sometimes narrowly perceived to be the "passing" on of knowledge from an "expert" to a "novice." You can probably remember many schooling experiences that consisted of teachers (and textbooks) holding those "right" answers and waiting for you to guess what was in their heads and pages—with their subsequent approval or dismissal of your answer. Critics such as Paolo Freire refer to this method as the "banking model" of education in which information is held like a valuable commodity by the teacher, passed to students in lectures and via textbooks, and then redeposited by students on multiple-choice and short-answer exams.

So what does this have to do with the writing process and tutoring? Well, writing is unique in how it functions. It fundamentally changes our relationship to whatever it is we are learning. Consider that the act of writing itself is often a process of discovery or of making meaning or, quite simply, of learning. The answers aren't predetermined by the teacher (at least not a good teacher) and cannot be corrected by running your paper through a Scantron machine (at least not yet). The concept of writing as a means of learning is fundamental to the writing process—and to writing centers.

Thus, it is important that you be reflective about your own writing process and understand the role of the tutor in writers' processes. These are some of the issues we'll address in this chapter.

WRITERS AND THE WRITING PROCESS

A bit of history: In the teaching of writing early in this century, students frequently wrote what were called "themes." The instructor wrote a topic on the blackboard and students dutifully went to work, crafting as carefully as they could an essay in response. These themes were collected, corrected (in red pen, of course), and returned. The expectation was that students would learn from daily practice and from the corrections their instructor made. Did students learn to write well from these methods? Perhaps some did, but not enough; this led the popular and academic press at the time to declare a "crisis" in students' communicative skills. As C. S. Duncan of Ohio State University wrote in 1914, "There is a spirit of unrest, a feeling of dissatisfaction in educational circles over the poor work done by students in English composition" (154). Blame was placed on teachers, families, and, most strongly, on the students themselves (particularly since such crises often coincide with increasing numbers of nonmainstream students coming to higher education). One solution at the time was to reconceive the teaching of writing as a "laboratory" course, akin to the scientific laboratory. Just as chemistry students conducted experiments in order to learn and apply the principles of chemistry, writing students would write in conditions that emphasized practice, guidance, and feedback (whether from peers or their teachers). Of course, much of this practice was in the service of having students make fewer mechanical errors (as early as 1895, John Franklin Genung of Amherst College described composition at his institution as "a veritable workshop, wherein, by systemized daily drill, details are mastered one by one" [174].), but the idea began to take hold that writing was an act that required practice and feedback, not simply the display of information in predetermined forms.

Fast-forward, 50 years or so (oftentimes ideas take hold slowly in higher education). By the 1970s, the idea of writing as a process took on a renewed importance as teachers and writers such as Peter Elbow, Janet Emig, Ken Macrorie, and Donald Murray became influential. In a time when the function of schooling was called into question (along with a host of other societal institutions), writing was "rediscovered" in a way, particularly as a way of making sense of one's experience and as a way of controlling one's own learning (or for "writing without teachers," as Peter Elbow told us in his influential book of the same name). Also around this time, educational psychology influenced the teaching of writing as researchers began to study the cognitive processes involved when one writes. Rather than just examining the habits of novelists and successful professional writers, researchers such as Janet Emig, Nancy Sommers, James Britton, Linda Flower, and John Hayes studied the ways that *students* wrote and described writing as a "recursive" act.[1] An additional strand was to reintroduce ideas from "classical" rhetoric and to look at the act of writing in terms of its rhetorical components, particularly the relationship between purpose, audience, and content. The confluence of these various movements turned into what Maxine Hairston has called "a paradigm shift," a virtual revolution in the way writing was conceived of and taught (albeit a "revolution" that was fomenting for 70 years or so!).

So what does this all mean for you as a writer and tutor? No doubt, in high school and college English classes, you've been exposed to notions of "stages" or "steps" in the writing process, whether called prewriting/writing/rewriting, gathering/drafting/revising (or a host of other labels and stages). Most important, we conceive of writing as a process, not a one-shot deal in a theme book, and we understand that a goal for any writer is to control his or her own process and to develop flexibility for approaching any writing task. These two notions—control and flexibility—seem to be opposites, but are, in fact, important contrasts, as we described in Chapter 1, and in a bit we will expand on each. Further, writing is now recognized as a "social act;" it isn't learned merely through drill-and-practice (which James Berlin calls the "current-traditional" approach to teaching writing); writing isn't completed in isolation by individual geniuses or used mainly to discover personal insight (the "expressivist" theory of writing); instead, writing and learning to write require us to interact with others (often called the "social-epistemic" or "social constructivist" theory of writing). As writing center theorist Andrea Lunsford writes, we need to view "knowledge and reality as mediated by or constructed through language in social use, as socially constructed, contextualized, as, in short, the product of *collaboration*" (4). Writing centers, therefore, are key components in this social view, as tutors and writers engage in one of the most powerful means of helping writers find and share meaning—collaborative talk.

Given that background, we now need to lay out some essentials of the writing process, ones that will probably seem quite familiar.

---

[1]Sondra Perl describes recursiveness: "…throughout the process of writing, writers return to substrands of the overall process, or subroutines (short successions of stops that yield results on which the writer draws in taking the next set of steps); writers use these to keep the process moving forward. In other words, recursiveness implies that there is a forward-moving action that exists by virtue of a backward-moving action." She goes on to say that writers might reread little bits of their writing, might return to a key word or topic, or they may pause and "look to their felt experience and [wait] for an image, a word, a phrase to emerge that captures the sense they embody." "Understanding Composing," *The Writing Teacher's Sourcebook*, ed. Gary Tate, Edward P. J. Corbett, Nancy Myers, 150–51.

A Model of the Writing Process

For several reasons, we want to provide you with a model of the writing process. As a writer, you can consider this model in light of how to approach any writing task. As a tutor, you can help writers by intervening in their writing processes, providing specific strategies, or helping them refine the strategies they already use.

However, several caveats are needed: First, models aren't intended to mirror reality. Instead, models are devices that begin to help us sketch a phenomenon, trace its rough edges, or simply begin to ask the questions we need to ask. Secondly, the model we'll describe is quite general—and a weakness of many models is that their generality obscures the importance of individual differences. That leads to our third caveat, one that's particularly important for the tutoring of writing: The writing process is an extremely idiosyncratic act. What works for you won't necessarily work for your closest friend or for a writer you're working with. The goal in applying the following model is to develop control and flexibility—those two contrasting notions we mentioned above. Finally, in the model, we'll describe a variety of strategies that you can both use as a writer and recommend as a tutor; however, in no way have we been exhaustive in our list of strategies. We do recommend that you find out more by consulting your writing center's handouts or the many complete texts on various writing strategies.

Our model of the writing process is based on the kinds of questions writers ask themselves at various points in the completion of any writing task and the strategies they might use to investigate those questions. We use three "episodes" in the writing process—planning, drafting, and revising—plus a fourth episode, proofreading/editing, more for simplicity's sake than anything else, but it's important to keep in mind the nonlinear shape of the writing process (one that's quite hard to render on paper). In other words, rather than steps or stages that one goes through one at a time, we conceive of the writing process as cyclical (or perhaps a vortex that sucks up all of your free time?!). You will often revisit the questions you first pose and the strategies you use to pursue them. Additionally, many things can influence the relative importance you attach to the various stages. For instance, writing a shopping list will require far less revising than writing a letter to the editor. And writing an essay analyzing an assigned reading you're not sure you even liked will take far more planning than a letter to a friend. Overall, we need to stress that context is everything. But first, let's finally describe the model. As you read this description, think about how closely it aligns to the process you use for school-based tasks:

Episode 1: Planning
Questions you might ask:

- What do I know about my topic?

- What is my purpose for writing?
- Who are my intended readers and how much do they know about my topic?
- How is this task like others I have had before?
- What structure will work best for my topic?

Strategies you might use to investigate these questions (not an exhaustive list!):

- Clustering: a visual representation of your thoughts on the topic, usually starting with a single word that invokes word associations, which you write around that first word, drawing a circle around each association and continually building until you've drawn a "cluster" of words (as conceived by Gabriel Rico).
- Freewriting: quick and exhaustive writing on the topic, often with a timed goal ("I'll write for five minutes without stopping.") and, as Peter Elbow tells us, likely to turn off your overwrought editor and tap into the generating portions of your brain.
- Conversation, either in class or with friends.
- Brainstorming: unstructured exploration of your ideas.
- Reading and research on your topic.

Overall, in this episode you're *trying* to answer the planning questions, not necessarily finding answers, and using the strategies that you feel will work best for your topic and task. Consider that a grocery list might come with a quick brainstorm or a conversation with a roommate or spouse, but an essay on the factors that contribute to the destruction of the Amazon Rainforest might require far more careful, extensive, and multistrategied planning.

Episode 2: Drafting
Questions you might ask:

- What do I know about my topic?
- What is my purpose for writing?
- Who are my intended readers and how much do they know about my topic?
- How is this task like others I have had before?
- What structure will work best for my topic?

Yes, we know, the questions are the same as for the first episode. That's our way of saying that, throughout your writing, you are working toward answering these questions. That is also why you might reuse the strategies we describe above. However, we feel there is one component in drafting that might not be as fully formed during planning—your *intention* or the feeling you get when you are trying to render on paper an idea or image or argument. You have an intention, usually quite out of focus in the early stages. Composition researchers Lil Brannon and Cy Knoblauch call this intention the "ideal text," as if you have a finished copy of your essay locked somewhere in your mind, and the point of this early writing is to find which strategy is the key to free that ideal text so that your rough drafts (your "real" text) will closely match the ideal. Brannon and Knoblauch are suspicious about this idea, particularly because "ideal texts" are often presented as absolutes by teachers or authority figures, with little room for students to challenge those ideas. We prefer to imagine that your intention as a writer and just how you'll go about putting that intention into words aren't necessarily complete in your mind. Instead, you need to use writing and language to bring a shape to your intentions. This is perhaps why it just feels so darn good to get something "right," to find the words to express your meaning. Thus, in the drafting episode of the composing process, you're doing some writing, perhaps lots of it, as you attempt to render your intentions on the page (or computer screen).

Strategies you might use when drafting:

- Any or all of those you used for planning.
- Outlining: Creating an outline can be particularly useful if you feel a strong loss of control—you have lots and lots to say, but need to figure out how you will present that material. However, outlines need to be flexible, not individual cages out of which your writing can never escape.
- Visual representations of your topic: We mentioned clustering as a planning strategy, but it's worth repeating here that if you have a strong sense of what you want to say, but not a clear sense of how all of those ideas will fit together, visually representing your work can be powerful. Sketch pads, black or white boards, floors filled with arranged piles of readings or notecards— anything that enables you to think visually can work here.

Episode 3: Revising
Questions you might ask:

- What do I know about my topic?
- What is my purpose for writing?
- Who are my intended readers and how much do they know about my topic?
- How is this task like others I have had before?
- What structure will work best for my topic?

Yes, at the risk of badgering, we know that we've repeated the questions again, but we wanted to emphasize the recursive nature of the writing process. By this episode, you have perhaps become satisfied with some of your answers to these questions. However, some might still remain underexplored. Revising is a vital episode for many reasons: First, some researchers (e.g., Beach; Faigley and Witte; Flower et al.; Sommers) have shown that revising is a crucial factor that separates successful writers from less successful ones. More significant, it has been our own experience that students often confuse revising with editing, our final episode. When you revise, you are making changes on a large scale, dealing with what Thomas Reigstad and Donald McAndrew call "higher-order concerns." This is when you realize that the "real" start of your essay is on page 3 and that you're better off saving the first two pages for another day. This is also when you realize that you've been repeating yourself on pages 2 and 4, and can perhaps group those parts together. And, finally, this is when you realize (and all of these realizations might come from your own reading of your drafts, a friend or peer's reading, or a writing center tutor's questions) that you simply need to develop one of your points more fully or flesh out a description or make much clearer just what your point is (and thus return to some planning strategies). Dealing with higher-order concerns is often what makes your writing go from good to great.

Contrast the moves above with what we'll call "later-order concerns,"[2] things such as fiddling with your wording, checking your spelling, making sure you've used "you're" instead of "your." These sorts of sentence-level fixes should come later in the process (though we won't claim that all writers don't fiddle with words and sentences as they draft; for less-experienced writers, however, the fiddling can subsume getting any real writing done). Also, sentence-level fixes are much more the province of editing than revising. They are certainly important and shouldn't be neglected, but an obsession with error should be avoided at all costs.

Strategies you might use when revising:

- Any or all of those you used for planning and drafting.
- Seeking feedback: We won't necessarily assume that, because you're learning to be a writing center tutor, you were a dutiful user of writing center services yourself (though we do hope so). Nevertheless, seeking feedback at any episode in the writing process is valuable, and revising is perhaps the point at which most writers seek feedback. Rather than imagine an intended reader, why not seek out a real one and find out if you're getting your point across?

---

[2]Reigstad and McAndrew call these "lower-order concerns"; however, we'll call them "later-order concerns" because we think that correctness is pretty important, especially to writers, and often to instructors.

- Glossing your text: An effective revising strategy we've found is to go back over our drafts, writing in the margins a brief (just a couple of words) description of each paragraph's content (we sometimes call this writing an outline in reverse). When you look at your descriptions, you can detect whether you've been repeating yourself. If your descriptions are difficult to write, you have an indication that your paragraph is unfocused or consists of too many topics. Your marginalia can also include not just the content of your paragraphs, but their function within sections or the essay as a whole. Now is the time you can discover that the paragraph you've marked "conclusion" contains an entirely new topic or that you're spending too much time on a single idea that's not central to your main point.

The Final Episode: Editing/Proofreading

Having made mention of later-order concerns, we would be remiss not to suggest some strategies for approaching editing/proofreading (and keep in mind that we'll discuss the important differences between editors and tutors in Chapter 3). Perhaps the best bit of advice we can offer is to edit in several passes with a different focus on each pass. For instance, you might read your text once just looking for spelling mistakes (and reading backwards—from the end to the beginning—can be helpful to force you to see each word in isolation). And then you might read your text looking only to shorten sentences and paragraphs, cutting out excess words. And then you might read focusing on the kinds of homonyms that have given you trouble (and the find/replace function of your word-processing software is great for this strategy).

One other strategy we offer writers in the writing center is to have them read their drafts aloud, if not to their tutors, then simply to themselves. Reading aloud forces you to *hear* your language, as well as to see errors that your eyes glossed over previously. Overall, the idea in editing/proofreading is to create some distance between yourself and your text or, more accurately, between what you've said and how you've said it. If you're still clarifying the point you are trying to make, you are revising. If you put that content aside and focus on the mechanics of your language, you are editing. This distinction is why we caution student writers to save editing for the very end of their process. Why fiddle with your mechanics when you might strike that entire sentence or paragraph in the service of clarifying your point?

TUTORS AND THE WRITING PROCESS

In no way have we been exhaustive in our list of strategies during each episode in the process (we encourage you to refer to the many books on these topics). One thing we do want to point out, however, comes back to the ideas of control and flexibility, one of those contrasts central to writing and to tutoring. Writers need to develop control of these strategies, and this control includes not simply knowing what strategies might be available, but knowing how to use a strategy. And then not just knowing what and how, but knowing when the use of a strategy would be appropriate (and this "strategic knowledge" concept comes from reading researchers Scott Paris, Margerie Lipson, and Karen Wixson). Our earlier example of outlining is a case in point. For years and years and still today in many textbooks, writing seemed to be a relatively simple process that started with choosing a topic and then writing an outline. However, we've worked with many frustrated writers in the writing center who told us, "I just cannot seem to come up with my thesis and outline." Well, that's not a surprise since they haven't created any material yet to find a focus or to organize into an outline. They simply didn't yet know what they wanted to say (content), much less how they would say it (structure). Applying the strategy of outlining at this point for these writers will lead to nothing but frustration. Instead, you can help these writers generate material in order to find a central focus. Brainstorming, mapping, clustering, or any of the strategies we described in Episode 1 would be useful. Once again, in terms of strategies, writers need to know the what, how, and when; they need to be flexible and adjust the way they work, depending upon a host of factors—the writing task itself, the conditions under which they are writing, the point of the process that they need to emphasize at that moment, and countless other things that make writing such a complex act.

Flexibility and control can be tied to an important concept that has grown out of work in cognitive psychology—the idea of "metacognition" or thinking about thinking. Consider how aware you are of your writing process. Do you need to think about how to get started when you're given a writing task? Do you consider the various prewriting strategies at your disposal and the appropriateness of each for what you are facing? No doubt, as a successful writer, you've given some thought to these questions, though you've probably internalized the answers to some degree. But in our work with less-successful writers, we've seen that issues of how well they know and can control the processes they use to write can be problematic. Thus, a goal for every writer is to develop strategic knowledge about each phase of the writing process, and writing center tutors can be a vital element in helping writers learn metacognitive control.

Perhaps the most important thing we can say about the writing process and your work as a tutor is this: Avoid creating clones of yourself; avoid teaching *your* processes as if they are the tried and true methods of approaching any writing task. Sure, they've worked for you as an English major (or sociology or business or biology or undeclared major), but that doesn't mean they'll necessarily work for another. Instead, as a tutor your goal should be to help writers develop control of and flexibility with their writing processes.

One clarification: We are not saying that you should never bring up the strategies you feel have been helpful to you. Remember that writers need to know *what* strategies are available. If you're a big fan of clustering and the writer has never tried it, pull out those big pieces of paper and have the writer cluster away. The same goes for any strategy. What's important is not to offer the strategy as a sure-fire solution; instead, you are helping writers develop their strategic repertoires. You can increase writers' options, teaching them what strategies are available, how to use those strategies, and the most appropriate time to apply a given strategy.

We've slipped somewhat into lecture mode here, but that's because the teaching of writing is fraught with instances of well-intentioned individuals simply applying the "teaching" methods that worked best for them (we've particularly seen this phenomenon when it comes to the teaching of grammar; "but *I* learned by diagramming sentences," they say.). This tendency is difficult to avoid, and that is one of the important reasons why you need to reflect deeply upon your own writing processes. Oftentimes, we aren't even aware of how prescriptive and controlling our teaching behaviors can be. Keep in mind that your goal is to create options for writers, not cut them off. And one of the many joys of tutoring is that *you* will learn, from writers, strategies that you had never considered before. Thus, an important line of inquiry that you can pursue in any tutoring session is to ask, "So, how did you go about writing this?"

One last point: Many writers don't necessarily ply their trade in response to assigned topics and in exchange for a grade or class credit. Those conditions are unique to writing in academic settings. And it is in those settings that the writing process and the tutor's role in that process need special consideration.

WRITING IN ACADEMIC SETTINGS

We've made the point a couple of times in this chapter that the writing process model that we offer is idealized. This quality is perhaps most true when it comes to the application of the model to writing in academic settings. Consider the questions about purpose and audience ("What is my purpose for writing? Who are my intended readers and how much do they know about my topic?"). If you are writing a paper for a class, on an obvious level your purpose is to complete an assigned task and your audience is your instructor. Of course, you might say that your purpose is to convince your reader of your point of view and your audience consists of your peers. However, in most instances, this audience won't be giving you a grade or sending your name in to the registrar at the end of the term in order for you to receive credit for the course. Most writing assignments are quite artificial, and your audience—your instructor—holds tremendous evaluative authority. These elements cannot help but powerfully affect the writing done in academic settings.

What we are addressing here is the relationship between the writer, the instructor, and the writer's text. Hopefully you have been lucky enough to feel "empowered" by the writing you have done. Your instructors haven't made the writing they've required merely a test of how well you've mastered the course content (not that there isn't a role for this sort of writing, but it's certainly a limited role). Instead, you've been able to use writing to make meaning, whether that means discovering and communicating how you feel about a significant event in your life, an important reading, or a topic you feel strongly about. And you've not just found meaning through writing, but you're able to share that meaning with others (your readers, of course)—connections that remind us how much we depend upon human fellowship.

However, some writers you might work with in the writing center won't be coming from such positive experiences. They fully realize that the purpose of their essay is to get a grade and eventually course credit, and that their audience is their powerful instructor. Thus, their expectation is that you help them figure out just what it is their instructor wants and how they can go about getting a decent grade.

Other writers, both native and nonnative English speakers, will seemingly be at a "cultural divide" from their instructors, their writing tasks, and, often, from you. Differences and cultural expectations due to language, ethnicity, gender, race, and class can often manifest themselves in something as "simple" as a paper due for a class. For instance, some students' writing closely resembles their speaking, and if these students speak with accents or in nonprivileged form, such as Black English, you might be put into the position of defending the implied values of academic writing—values that stem from largely Western, male, and Caucasian influences. Before you know it, you will be assuming a "regulatory role," as Nancy Grimm calls the function of writing centers, often inadvertently, to manage difference and act as an enforcement mechanism for the status quo.

Now, rather than have you resign your tutoring job before you get started, we want to point out that these dilemmas, while vital and complex, are also best managed by acting in ways that we recommend throughout this book: being sensitive to writers' backgrounds and challenges, asking questions about the writers' tasks and their understanding of those tasks, and working to create options for writers, not to close off those possibilities. In Chapter 4, we'll delve more deeply into those often assumed expectations that you and writers will bring to a writing center session and how they can affect your work.

RENT TO OWN

A notion central to writing center work is that writers need to "own" their texts. In Chapter 3, we draw a distinction between editing—something that perhaps many of your classmates have sought from you because they recognized your writing abilities—and tutoring. As we have discussed, many writers might come to the writing center under the impression that a tutor will simply fix their texts. We often call this the "dry-cleaner" model of writing center, and unfortunately have had more than a few writers ask us if they could drop off their papers and then return when they were "done." However, tutors don't fix texts; we teach writers how to fix texts. We don't tell writers what to write; we ask questions about and react as readers to what writers have already written or are thinking of writing. In these ways, writers "own" their texts, and writing center workers respect this ownership just as we would want it for ourselves.

Nevertheless, the student-text-teacher relationship complicates notions of ownership. For many writers, a more accurate concept would be that they "rent" their texts, occupying a topic and content for the length of time specified by the teacher/landlord, and thinking little of what they have written once the rental period has ended. This is perhaps why we have had writers tell us flat out in writing center sessions that they plagiarized much of their research papers or that they "hate to write" but know that they need to overcome the "burden" of a required writing course. Writing is not meaningful for these writers because they have never had the experience of its meaning (in school, at least; we've also seen that some of the most reluctant writers in our classes are avid private writers, keeping journals and writing poetry that they would never share). Do these writers "own" the writing they are doing in their classes?

For the writing center tutor, these issues certainly complicate neat renderings of the writing process. At times, writers will position you as proxies for their instructors, expecting an evaluation of their writing. At others, they will put you in the role of "coconspirator," especially when they admit plagiarizing or simply not caring about what they're writing. What is important is that you are aware of the writing process—especially the ideas of control and flexibility—and how writing in academic settings affects that process. As a student yourself, you know best what it means to write in academic settings, and can best impart to those you work with in the writing center the strategies that are effective.

It is our experience that most writers are eager to find meaning in what they write, even if the task wasn't best designed to achieve that end. And one of the great pleasures in writing center work is helping writers find that meaning. Your knowledge of the writing process will be vital in providing that help.

3

THE TUTORING PROCESS

In this chapter, we want to take you through the entire tutoring process—from opening a session to closing one—and lay out some good tutoring strategies. We'll expand upon these strategies in subsequent chapters as we take you from anticipating (Chapter 4), observing (Chapter 5), and then participating in sessions, first with your fellow trainees (Chapters 6 and 7), and then on your own (Chapter 8). We'll also offer ways to think about specific situations you'll encounter: helping students with their reading (Chapter 9), helping non-native English speakers (Chapter 10), analyzing your sessions (Chapter 11), working on-line with writers (Chapter 12), maintaining an ethical framework (Chapter 13), and, finally, troubleshooting those many difficult situations that all tutors encounter (Chapter 14).

We'll frame our overview of the tutoring process by showing how tutors approach each stage of a session, and contrast that with what editors might do in the same situation. As we mentioned in chapter 1, one of the most important contrasts in writing center work is the difference between editing and tutoring. You are probably already a skilled editor, and your services are in demand from friends and classmates. Also, by no means do we want to denigrate the good work that many editors do (after all, you might choose that career); however, writing center work is based upon the belief that writers need to do the writing, not their tutors. Like any of the contrasts we presented, the tutor/editor one is on a continuum, and there'll probably be instances outside of the writing center where you'll be closer to the editing end (and hopefully be paid for that challenging service). In the writing center, though, we advise you to tutor, not to edit; after all, it's the writer whose name is going on that paper, who's paying for those credits, and who'll be getting the grade. But before we get too strident, we need to define in more detail the differences between editing and tutoring.

When you think of an editor, you might think of a cranky, hard-bitten, cigar-chomping Perry White, calling all the shots and making all the decisions, sending Clark Kent and Lois Lane off on assignments. Or you might think of someone who is responsible for making someone else's good writing perfect—that is, a proofreader. Real editors of various kinds probably wouldn't like these stereotypes of their work, but these descriptions come close to what a lot of friends do when they are asked to look over a paper. That is, your friend hands over the paper, picks up your last slice of pizza, and loses himself in *Days of Our Lives* while you go to work with a pen or a pencil.

You might limit your "looking over" of the paper to proofreading, and this usually involves making corrections for your friend; it may go beyond proofreading and involve suggesting a better word or a better sentence; it may even involve some advice: "I had a class with her, and she always wants you to...." When you do this kind of editing for your friends, you are assuming a level of control over their paper (and often they want you to). For tutors, however, this control can squelch any real learning on the writer's part.

THE TUTOR DOES NOT—AND DOES— HAVE TO BE AN EXPERT

An important difference between editors and tutors has to do with the idea of being an "expert." Editors are often seen as expert wordsmiths, always knowing the right word, the correct grammatical fix, or the key passage to delete. The writers you work with might indeed put you in this role, just as some of your friends might have, but tutoring expertise is quite different.

As a tutor, you don't have to be an expert on the subject matter of the paper the writer is working on, and you don't even have to be an expert on grammar and correctness—knowing that something isn't right is probably enough (though having a good working knowledge of English grammar and usage can often be helpful, particularly with non-native English speakers who will know those rules quite well). But you do have to be an expert in some things, each of which we'll explain in more detail in this chapter: knowing how to set a good tone for the conference and making the writer feel comfortable; knowing which kinds of issues to address first; being patient and listening to the entire paper, since it's easy to get hung up on an early section when the real challenge might come later; knowing how to ask questions that are open-ended (not questions that can be answered with a yes or no) and that are ones you really want answers to and don't know already; knowing techniques that let the writer make the decisions; knowing that sometimes our questions take time to answer and having the patience to wait for the writer to come up with a reply; and knowing that when the writer revises, many of the problems with correctness will improve.

As a tutor, rather than as an editor, you'll have to know when more is needed—that is, when there are so many problems that you can't deal with them all in one session—and you'll have to know what to do with students who can't complete everything. You'll have to get a sense that with some writers, you can't address every last problem in the paper, and you'll have to be able to choose one or two to begin with, but then encourage the writer to come for more help. You'll have to know when a writer needs to come back after revision to work on correctness. You'll know that scheduling another appointment at the end of the session is a good way to help the writer stick to her resolve to revise and that the next session should be with you again, if schedules permit. You'll have to be sensitive to due dates; if the writer only has an hour, she may appreciate knowing that she needs to rethink her organization, but chances are she won't be able to do much about it, so you and she can focus on correctness, but you'll also have to know that it's a good idea to invite her back so she'll have a better sense of how to organize and what effect organization has on readers.

All of that is a lot to learn. But as you see, being an expert on grammar didn't even come up. And the writer is responsible for being the expert on her subject matter. If you know the subject well, that's wonderful, but if you don't, it's all right. You can still tell what kind of paper is appropriate, whether or not the arguments are well-supported, if the organization is clear to you, and whether the audience is being addressed in an effective way.

Nevertheless, we do need to mention that there are times that disciplinary expertise will be important. For example, a writing tutor who is a biology major will have much more knowledge of how to approach writing up scientific data than would someone who's never had to approach that task. And a business major will know more about the specifics of writing a business plan than would a theology major; in other words, depending upon your major and your experience, you might have specific knowledge about the writing conventions of particular majors or disciplines. Now, this isn't to say that, as a tutor, you'll merely tell the writers, "No, the results of your experiments do not go in your methods section." Instead, you'll have even greater knowledge of the important questions to ask than would a more "general" tutor: "Why did you put your results in the methods section? How have other writers dealt with that placement in some of the research articles you've read?" Your goal is still to let writers control their own work, but your expertise in these matters can be quite valuable. Many writing centers have recognized this value and recruit tutors—often graduate students—from a wide variety of majors, encouraging writers to "match up" with someone in their discipline. But we also want to repeat a warning: As a tutor, rather than an editor, your job isn't to offer content expertise and launch into a protracted lecture on the roots of the Russian Revolution. You need to respect writers' need to discover—with your help—the information they need to clarify a point or expand an argument.

START WITH QUESTIONS

So, you're on your first shift in the writing center and ready to help that first eager writer, paper clutched in his hand. What do you do? Think about the way you might "look over" a friend's paper when you are in the role of editor. Chances are, you take the paper and probably go off with it, perhaps somewhere quiet, where you can concentrate.

As a tutor, you're going to do this process differently. We train our tutors to start by asking writers a few basic questions before they even consider the draft:

- What was the assignment?
- What is your central point or main argument? (We don't say "what is your thesis?" or the writer is likely to read us a sentence that won't help us much. Besides, when the writer sums the paper up and we write that down, sometimes the summary is a better thesis than the one in the paper. We can then help the writer see that, so write down the paraphrase for later.)
- What concerns you, or what do you want me to pay careful attention to? (And we write this down, because we'll surely come back to it later, and either reassure the writer, or address the issue that's raised.)

After you write those answers down, you're ready to work with the writer on the draft.

READING ALOUD

The next step is probably a major shift from what you're used to doing: We recommend that you ask the writer to read the paper aloud to you while you take notes. If you've never done this before, we know that this idea takes some getting used to. But think of the action of taking your friend's paper and going off with it or writing on it. You're in control. You're calling the shots. And the writer, who in a writing center is probably someone you don't know, someone who doesn't have your pizza to eat and doesn't have a TV handy, so if you were to read silently, there would be an awkward moment as he waits for your "diagnosis." That metaphor from medicine comes too easily to mind for this to be a good thing, we think.

When the writer reads the paper, he accomplishes several things, in addition to keeping in control. As you listen, you make a mental note not to interrupt, except to ask him to repeat something you didn't catch, and you listen to the whole paper. Listening to the whole thing from start to finish and taking notes puts you in the role of the learner, and the writer in the role of the expert. And while we can't swear to this, our anecdotal evidence is pretty good that the reader is listening, too, to the way the draft is working. Sometimes he'll pause and make a mark in the margin. Sometimes he'll say "Oh, that sounds bad," and you can say, "Put a checkmark next to it and we'll come back to it." But he's giving his draft a critical reading in ways that will help him revise, and this is what we want.

You're taking notes, listening. As we've already pointed out, he's the expert, since it's his paper. We talked about the editor's making all the final decisions, but in a good tutorial, the tutor asks questions, and the writer decides what to do with a draft.

AN EXAMPLE OF OPENING A TUTORING SESSION

Because what we've described up to this point is so important, we include the following transcript as an example (and we recommend that you read it aloud, preferably with a partner taking the second speaking role). This excerpt comes from the beginning of a session and starts with the writer asking for general feedback on her paper, and then the tutor asks about what the writer is working on:

Writer: This is an analytical paper.

Tutor: Okay.

Writer: It's basically regarding a reading passage assigned in the class, and we're supposed to do a critique on that.

Tutor: Okay. And two things: First, what was the reading passage?

Writer: The reading passage was "The Tourist," by Jamaica Kincaid.

Tutor: Jamaica Kincaid, yeah, I know her, but I don't know that [piece]. Was it an entire essay or just a passage from an essay?

Writer: Actually it was a short essay.

Tutor: Mm, hmm. And when you say critique it, what is your conception of what that involves, what that task involves?

Writer: Well, I'm supposed to take a stand, whether I agree with her or I have a different opinion, and I guess I have a different opinion.

Tutor: Okay. So tell me two things, what was her position?

Writer: She doesn't like tourism…because she comes from a different country, I guess.

Tutor: Yeah.

Writer: And she doesn't like tourists going to her country because they ex-ploit her country in such a way.

Tutor: Mm, hmm. That's her main reason?

Writer: Right.

Tutor: Because it constitutes exploitation? And does she give examples of the exploitation, what that might look like?

Writer: Well, in the paper I have some of her viewpoints but, and then basi-cally she says that, at the very end she says that the natives, every native would like to travel, that's for sure, but most of the natives in this world are very poor and so they are not able to, they cannot afford to go to other coun-tries, so they would envy you and the fact that you, as a tourist, come to their country, it makes them jealous more.

Tutor: Mm, hmm. So her audience is, the readers she has in mind, sounds like those who would be tourists?

Writer: Right.

Tutor: I'll tell you what, will you read it to me? Reading's a good way, you can tell me, in a sense, what I should listen for, what your concerns are with this draft. And reading it out loud is a good way for you to get a feel for how it's shaping up, what your language is like.

Writer: Okay.

Notice several things in this excerpt about what the tutor does. He doesn't just ask about what the assignment is (an "analytical paper," according to the writer), but he also probes further by asking questions. What did the writer have to read (and notice that the tutor immediately acknowledges that he's not familiar with the reading passage, thus putting the writer into the position of "teaching" him the essay's content)? What is the writer's con-ception of an "analytical" paper? And once she describes that task ("I'm sup-posed to take a stand, whether I agree with her or have a different opinion."), he asks more questions to preview the paper itself: What is the author's po-sition? What evidence does she present to support that position? Who seems to be the author's intended audience—whom is she trying to persuade?

These questions accomplish several things: They probe the writer's un-derstanding of the assigned task and of the reading itself. They also intro-duce some of the elements of a "critique" essay: a summary of the author's main claim, a presentation of her evidence, and a sense of her intended au-dience. Once the writer gives this information, it provides the foundation for what will happen once the writer reads the paper itself, a means of checking back on whether or not the writer has included these elements and is consistent with what she told her tutor, compared with what she wrote.

Notice, too, that the tutor asks the writer to read her work aloud, giving a short justification. Thus, in this passage the tutor establishes his responsibilities: to ask about the task and the context, to help the writer better understand the task, and to evaluate how well the writer fulfills her stated purpose. Overall, he's putting himself in the position of "reader" of her essay, making as visible as possible what he'll be expecting and listening for as she reads her essay aloud.

Now consider that the dialogue above took up only about two-and-a-half minutes! The first few minutes of a session are crucial to establish a rapport with the writer, set goals, and lay a foundation for what next occurs. In the exchange that time was brief, but what occurred was certainly crucial to the success of the session as a whole.

HIGHER-ORDER CONCERNS COME FIRST

Okay, you've started the session with questions, you've taken notes, and the writer has read her paper aloud; now what do you do? One way to create the right atmosphere is for you first to comment on something you like in the paper (and this is a major contrast between the work of tutors and what editors do). We all want praise, and the writers with whom you'll work make themselves quite vulnerable by sharing their writing with you. However, don't push it. Writers will know if you're being phony and will feel patronized. But there's generally something good in every piece of writing. Find it. If words fail you, you can comment (if this is true), "Wow. You've really done a lot of work on this." Or "You've really done a good job of finding research sources," or "Great topic." But only say those things if they're true for you.

As we mentioned in talking about the writing process, one of the most important things you can do as a tutor is to deal first with what Thomas Reigstad and Donald MacAndrew call higher-order concerns. As a tutor, you'll save grammar and correctness for later (and, as we noted in Chapter 2, we'll call these matters later-order concerns). Higher-order concerns are the big issues in the paper, ones that aren't addressed by proofreading or editing for grammar and word choice. This isn't to say that proofreading isn't important for writers to learn, but we can tell you that, from our experience, if we help writers proofread first, a lot of writers—especially those who are inexperienced or hesitant—won't want to change anything in their papers, even to make things better, because they feel that once they have their sentences and punctuation right, all will be well with their writing (and perhaps you felt this way as well at some point in your writing history).

When dealing with higher-order concerns, you'll think about such questions as:

- Is the writer really addressing the assignment and fulfilling its terms?
- Is there a need for a thesis, and if so, is there one?
- Do arguments have the support they need? Is there an organization I can relate to as a reader? Is this piece addressing an audience in an effective way?
- Does the piece show appropriate levels of critical thinking?

In the ideal world (where writing tutors would be out of a job!), we'd answer these questions with yes, yes, yes, yes, yes, and yes. But quite often the answer is no, and then we have a focus for our session.

Let's say the draft has some problems that the questions above will identify. As an editor, you would tell the writer what to do. You'd tell the writer that she needs a thesis, and maybe you'd suggest one to her. You might even write one for her. But that's not necessarily what's best for the writer.

In his well-known essay "The Idea of a Writing Center," Stephen North says, "[I]n a writing center the object is to make sure that writers, and not necessarily their texts, are what get changed.... [O]ur job is to produce better writers, not better writing" (438). As we pointed out, you're probably already a good editor and might have lots of good ideas for ways to improve the papers you'll be seeing, but it's better for the writer if she makes the decisions about the paper. Making decisions gives the writer a better sense of ownership of the paper, and more pride in it when revisions go well. This emphasis on ownership will prompt us to ask questions not only about the paper in question, but about the writer's processes of composing:

- How many drafts has she written?
- What kind of revising has she done?
- Have any classmates or her teacher read any of the drafts and offered any advice?
- How does she feel about the advice?
- What are her revising strategies? (Does she have any?)

Some students who come to the writing center have never really and truly revised a paper and have no idea how to go about rethinking a subject or even how to move paragraphs around; you need to find out how comfortable the writer is with these moves. Sometimes it's good to ask the questions about revising at the end of the session, when the writer has a sense that she may need to make some sweeping changes.

If we see an organization that seems odd to us, we might ask the writer, "What made you put this section on X right here between this section on A and this one on B?" When we ask such questions, we're showing the writer that we trust her decisions. Maybe there's a connection that we didn't see. If we didn't see it, and the writer explains it, we can ask if some sort of explanation or clarification belongs in the draft, or what's more likely, the writer will say, "Oh, I need to make that clear, don't I?"

There are lots of good questions we can keep handy for tutorials. One of the best ones was a suggestion of one of our tutors, Dan Giard. Dan always likes to ask, right after the writer has read the draft, "Now that you hear it again, what do you want to do with it next?" This keeps the writer in the role of expert (and after all, she's likely to have done plenty of research on her topic; if not, and if it's needed, you need to ask more questions about the content). Another good question starts with a thumbnail sketch of the organization of the essay as you heard it and as you took notes about it. Then, the question is simply, "Is this what you wanted me to get out of your paper?"

These questions show that we trust the writer and the writer's decisions. We're not trying to take over the writing process. We're trying to help the writer see what kinds of questions she should be asking of her own paper. If we model these questions for the writer, then it's our hope that next time, she will ask them herself.

WHAT IF THERE'S NO ESSAY?

If you've had any experience with a writing center (maybe you've visited yours as a writer already), you know that not all sessions start with a draft of a paper. Writing center directors do a lot of public relations trying to let writers know that the earlier in the process they come in, the better they are helped. You probably know from your own experience how helpful it is to talk over your assignments with your friends, classmates, or instructors before you ever do any writing. And once you start writing, you know how your ideas can take shape if you just take time to talk them over again. This is another kind of help we offer as tutors and that contrasts with the work of editors.

A good way to begin such a session as this is to have the writer paraphrase the assignment for you. This will give you a really good sense of how well he knows what's expected of him. If he's stumbling around and pulls out an assignment sheet, that could mean he's having a hard time just understanding what's expected. You can help here, looking over the sheet with him, explaining what you think the assignment is asking for, and encouraging him to clarify any ambiguous points with his instructor.

You know from your own experience that you'll write the best papers on topics you care about, so it's good to help the writer identify parts of the assignment that are meaningful or that draw from his life experiences in some way or that touch on subjects he may be interested in as he plans his career. Sometimes writers find topics that simply fascinate them, and they will write well about them, because they want to know more and because they want to share what they know.

Sometimes writers come to us with a lack of trust in their own perceptions of things. Many schools begin with an assignment that asks them to relate their experiences, asking questions such as "Write about a time when writing went really well for you" or "Describe an experience that changed you." Inexperienced writers can be very uncomfortable with those assignments, because many of them have been taught "Never use first person," or "Never give your opinion. Just the facts." They have to unlearn these rules, and talking about the assignment can help them warm up to these writing tasks. The research paper will come soon enough, in most schools.

As we pointed out in Chapter 2, there are a variety of ways that you can help writers generate material or figure out what it is they want to say. We like to help writers get their first thoughts and preconceptions out of the way by writing them down. (Peter Elbow and Pat Belanoff call this Loop Writing.[1]) Now you can point your questions toward refinements of those first thoughts. Lots of beginning writers will go with those first thoughts and use them to base a paper on; however, for most college assignments, this won't be good enough. They will probably be common knowledge, certain to put the instructor to sleep. As a tutor, you can ask the writer what interests him most about those ideas he's generated already. What would he like to know more about? Does he know how to find good research sources? Or does the assignment call for him to write about his own experiences?

HELPING WITH LATER-ORDER CONCERNS

Imagine that all those higher-order concerns are fine in a writer's draft, but there are some errors; or imagine that you've already spent a session or two on the higher-order concerns and can now address later-order concerns. How do you know there are errors if you've only listened to the writer read the paper? Chances are that you don't, unless you heard some awkward sentences (the ones that just didn't make sense to you) and unless you heard the writer misuse some words. To address later-order concerns, you have to *see* the paper. We suggest that you sit next to the writer for this process, and *you're* going to reread the essay, perhaps now reading one sentence or para-

---

[1]They then have writers develop either moments, stories, or portraits, then generate some dialogue; then they have them vary their audience or chronology; and then they have them think of lies, errors, or sayings about the topic. Some of these techniques will be more valuable than others, depending on the assignment.

graph at a time. Once again, we're going to trust the writer. Maybe this time you'll read the paper aloud as you both look it over, but instead of going all the way through it, you'll stop when you spot an error or think you do. In your editor role, you'd have corrected the error. But tutors have better ways of helping students, ways that make them better writers.

Many sentence-level problems are not the result of a writer's carelessness or lack of understanding about correctness; instead, all of us will often write confusing sentences when we're trying to convey ideas that are particularly complex or only partially formed in our minds, or when we're writing in ways that we're really not familiar with (as in writers who tell us, "I've never written a critique essay and have no idea how to approach it."). Few writers get it right the first time, but many have the capability to correct their sentence-level problems with your help; rather than acting as an editor, you'll be teaching writers techniques so they can become good editors. An example of this technique is to say, "There's a sentence in the middle, in that paragraph about…that confuses me. Could you paraphrase it for me?" Write down what the writer says. Chances are that the paraphrase will be clear, because there's a clear context for it and a specific audience (you) that makes it easier for the writer to be clear. Then you can give feedback: "I really understood what you just said." Show the writer what you wrote down—and be sure not to correct or to add your own words to it, but keep it in the writer's own words. You might ask about the writing process at this stage, and see if the writer can reflect a bit on what was going on during the composition of the unclear sentence. Sometimes she will be able to see what she needs to do to make things clearer.

For a writer whose entire paper was full of unclear sentences, we've tape-recorded the entire tutoring session. She'd read a sentence, paraphrase it, and move on quickly, and we then loaned her the tape. Writers are very grateful for that kind of help.

ERROR ANALYSIS

We often find that new tutors are most terrified by the idea of a writer's paper that is just full of errors. Where do you start? Well, as we've emphasized, you start with higher-order concerns, but there will come a time when you'll need to help writers work to correct those repeated errors and become better editors of their own work. Composition researchers such as Mina Shaughnessy and David Bartholomae have given us a great deal of insight into the study of errors that writers make. Most important, you need to view errors not as manifestations of carelessness or sloth or stupidity but instead as stages in any writer's development. So what does this mean for you as a tutor? Well, trying to understand the logic behind a writer's errors is perhaps the most important help you can offer. While editors wield red pens and circle errors like stains on the page, tutors try to get at the reasons why writers made the choices they did. This process isn't particularly different from the way you addressed higher-order concerns. You asked what the writer already knew about the sort of essay she had to write or you asked about why she ordered the paragraphs in the manner she did or chose particular details, and then you tried to build upon that prior knowledge. With error analysis, you'll take the same approach to comma use or subject-verb agreement or sentence boundaries. Your most powerful question for the writer is, "Why did you make that choice?"

One other important strategy in error analysis is to look for patterns. As you read through the essay, perhaps a paragraph at a time, you can look for certain types of errors that the writer makes repeatedly. A common example is a comma splice or two independent clauses joined with only a comma (and we've also found that writers are often quite aware of the types of errors they make since they've been told repeatedly that they have that "problem" but often aren't shown how to correct it). Imagine that you are reading the paragraph and see several instances of comma splices. Your best bet is to ask the writer, "Why did you put this comma here?" While this is sort of a leading question (and most writers will reply, "Is that wrong?"), many will explain a logic behind the comma placement, perhaps that they felt that the clauses on each side of the comma were short or closely related or that they heard a pause at that spot and thought the rule with commas was to put one wherever they paused in their writing. Sometimes a writer will have memorized rules that are wrong.

At that point, you would tell him that it's an error, let's say, to put a comma between independent clauses. You may need to explain the idea of the independent clause to him, perhaps looking the concept up in a handbook. Referring to the handbook is a good idea if you know something is wrong but don't have the answer at your fingertips, and it also models a behavior we want writers to imitate: to go for the handbook and look up the rule.

In more step-by-step form, error analysis looks like the following:

1. You see an error. First, you want to know if the writer spots it and can correct it. So you ask, "Do you see an error in this sentence?" Chances are that the writer will find and correct it without any problem. But let's say that the writer doesn't see it. Then we get to the next step.

2. Talk about the general class of errors, saying, "The problem is with your verb, " or "There's a punctuation error." Give the writer time to spot it, and if he still doesn't see it, it is time for the next step.

3. Point out the error to him. "The problem is with this comma." Ask about the writer's logic behind making the error. See if he knows how to fix it. If not, ask him what rule he used to decide to put a comma where he did. As we noted above, writers often misinterpret or misapply rules. If the writer still hasn't made the correction, proceed to the next step.

4. Explain the specific rule (and refer to the handbook, as we pointed out) and have the writer apply it to his error. Help him make the fix if you need to, but explain as thoroughly as you can why you're making the choices that you made.

5. Go on to the next example of this error, but try and have the writer apply what you've taught in the previous example. And then treat each error in this fashion. For many writers, you'll soon not need even to point out the problem; they will recognize and fix the error on their own.

As you can see, error analysis can be a slow process and completely different from telling the writer what to do (as an editor would). As an effective tutor, you're having the writer do as much of the work as possible and teaching the writer the ways to correct errors. If you've noted patterns of errors, we advise you not to deal with more than three different types in a single tutoring session. That's all you'll have time and energy for, and it's all most writers can learn to correct in one session.

Another important role you can play in error analysis is not to focus just on errors but to find and point out instances where the writer has made correct choices. For instance, in the case of a writer who has a few comma splices, like the one we described above, you then see that there is a sentence where he has punctuated two independent clauses correctly. Point it out to him. It's a process of giving positive reinforcement, not just of finding errors, and you want to maintain the good rapport you have established with the writer, not come across as a representative of the "grammar police."

ENDING THE SESSION

A good session will fly by, so you'll have to be very aware of time. If there's no clock where you tutor, have a watch handy. It's often a good idea to offer the writer something such as, "We have ten minutes left; do you still want to talk about the five pages we haven't looked at or is there another priority we should address?" When the time is almost up, it's a good idea to get a sense of what the writer got out of the session. "What do you plan to do next?" is a good question to ask. As the writer tells you, you can encourage him to write those plans down. If a lot more remains to be done, you'll want to schedule another appointment, or maybe even two, if your center allows that. Schedule those appointments with you if at all possible, because you know the assignment, you know the writer's revision plans (and you'll keep a record of that), and you'll be able to jump right into the session without a lot of explanations. You're also building a relationship with the writer, and you want him to feel comfortable about coming back to you with this or other writing projects.

AFTER THE SESSION

Most writing centers require that you be ready for your next session, and most ask you to write down some notes on the session you've just completed. Sometimes this is a note for instructors, and sometimes it's just a memo for the next tutor this writer may work with ("We worked on a paper on jet lag. We looked at his organization and he clarified for me how he meant it to be set up. He'll reorganize it, get more research, and come back on Wednesday"). Always be aware of your audience with these notes. If the writer has any access to them, be sure there are no notes you'd be embarrassed to have him see. You'll have to be sure you leave time to do this between sessions, because believe it or not, after three sessions with writers, you're likely to have forgotten a lot about the first two.

EDITORS VERSUS TUTORS—A SUMMARY

What we've described about the tutoring process is very different from what went on in the TV lounge of your residence hall as those friendly neighborhood editors went about their business. We'll end by summarizing the contrast between tutors and editors:

Editors	Tutors
Focus on the text	Focus on the writer's development and establish rapport
Take ownership of the text	Make sure the writer takes ownership
Proofread	Start with higher-order concerns and worry about correctness last
Give advice	Ask questions
Read silently	Ask the writer to read aloud
Look mainly for things to improve	Comment on things that are working well
Work with an ideal text	Trust the writer's idea of a text
Make corrections on the page	Keep hands off and let the writer make corrections; help them learn correctness
Tell writers what to do	Ask them their plans for revision

4

EXAMINING EXPECTATIONS

When you attend a class, what do you consider to be your responsibilities? To arrive on time? To be prepared? To take notes in response to what your teacher says or writes? And what do you consider to be your teacher's responsibilities—also to arrive on time and be prepared? To "stimulate" learning? To respect you and your fellow students? Where do you believe your expectations for these responsibilities come from?

Just as in classrooms, in writing center sessions, you and the writers with whom you'll work bring expectations about each of your responsibilities, and each of you will also bring goals for the session. When goals and expectations reasonably agree, the work of the tutorial can go on relatively smoothly. When the goals and expectations clash, however, you're left feeling pretty awful. Something didn't work. Was it your fault? The writer's fault?

In this chapter, we focus on the goals and expectations that you will undoubtedly bring to your tutoring (and to your observation of others' tutoring) and how your preconceived notions about many of the contrasts that define tutoring—tutor versus editor, peer versus teacher, writer versus writing—are powerful influences that you and writers might not even be aware of. We'll discuss how those expectations might have been formed, and why it's necessary to reflect deeply upon what has shaped your expectations for behavior. In particular, we'll focus on two powerful influences: (1) your culturally based expectations for the "rules" of communication, and (2) your influential teaching/learning experiences. We will also introduce you to Adria, a graduate student in Applied Linguistics and a writing center tutor. We'll describe how Adria's expectations for effective tutoring—largely the result of her student experiences—manifested themselves in her sessions as a fairly nonflexible approach and became a source for nonproductive tutoring.

We need to stress that it is perfectly natural for your experiences to guide the expectations you'll bring to tutoring. This is a key process in learning. Here's how linguist Deborah Tannen puts it:

> *The only way we can make sense of the world is to see the connections between things, and between present things and things we have experienced before or heard about. These vital connections are learned as we grow up and live in a given culture. (14)*

However, what would not be ideal would be for your connection between old and new to turn into inflexible rules and summary judgments, rather than your carefully listening and observing to discover how the new experience differs from the old one. Our goal in this chapter is for you to develop control and flexibility, that important contrast we described in regard to your writing process. Becoming an effective tutor will often mean transcending your expectations and opening up communication so that you and the writer have a clear sense of what you both can accomplish in a session, as well as how and why.

COMMUNICATION BREAKDOWN

We all have cultural expectations for behavior, particularly those that have to do with communication (and we use culture here to refer to those influences based on race, ethnicity, religion, gender, and class). It is quite likely that many writers you'll work with will not share your cultural experiences or will attach different value than you do to certain kinds of behavior. Whether this means a writer who refuses to make eye contact or one who sits more closely than is comfortable for you, it is essential that you don't condemn these behaviors simply because they are different from what you value. Instead, you need to reflect upon what it is you're observing and why you're making certain interpretations and judgments.

Observation and reflection are not the only thing that tutoring requires, however. After all, you will be a participant in the activity that occurs. You will be enacting the "social rules" that govern all interaction. As an example, consider a conversation you've had recently with a friend. Both you and your friend have internalized the various rules each of you follows to ensure that your conversation flows along, isn't too awkward, and achieves the goals each of you has (for example, to learn or tell some new information or to solidify your friendship). These rules include those involving turn-taking (and you probably have had conversations where two people spoke at once—not very productive!) and maintaining the topic or at least moving on to tangents with some sense of agreement. Consider the verbal cues you or your friend might have used to signal that the other should keep talking ("Uh huh," "Yeah," "I know what you mean.") and the verbal signals to indicate it's the other person's turn to speak ("That reminds me of something I needed to tell you," "What do you think of that?"). Many years of conversations within particular cultures have made these rules something you don't even think about—except when they are violated.

In a tutoring session, social rules for the interaction apply just as much as for conversations (and we'll supply much more depth on how to analyze the discourse of a session in Chapter 11). As a tutor, you need to pay particular attention to the rules for behavior that you and the writer seem to be relying on. For writers new to the writing center, meeting with a tutor might be more akin to meeting with a classroom teacher than with a peer, and their behaviors might position you as much more of an authority figure than you might expect. Or, perhaps, the opposite might occur, and the writer might approach your session much more casually than you would wish. In either case, both you and the writer have certain expectations for behavior, expectations that arise out of your experiences with similar situations.

Instances of cross-cultural communication can particularly mark clashes between expectations for social rules. After all, your notions of the "right" way to act in a social situation are largely products of your culture, and you won't always share cultural expectations with writers. That does not mean that your tutorial with a writer from a culture different from your own will be marked by awkwardness, confusion, and frustration. Instead, our point is that as an effective tutor, you need to try to understand why some interactions simply do not "feel" right—including sessions you just observe and those you play a part in. When you hear a fellow tutor come out of a writing center session saying, "That really didn't go well. We just didn't click," think about the sort of clues—both verbal and physical—that you could observe to explain that feeling. Just as in conversation, who speaks when and who controls the topic play an important role in tutoring sessions, as do how you and the writer sit in relation to each other, where the writer's paper is positioned, the noise level of the room, and a host of other factors.

A QUESTION OF GOALS

Expectations for the "rules" of interaction are just one influence on the outcome of your sessions. You and the writers will also bring goals for your sessions, and one of the many tricky parts of tutoring is not only uncovering your own goals (which aren't always as visible as you think), but negotiating with the writer on a mutually agreeable goal. This "agenda setting" during the first five minutes of a session is perhaps the most crucial of all. The "classic" example of a clash of goals is the writer who is interested primarily in getting his paper "fixed" (and, after all, who can blame writers for wanting better papers to be the result of their writing center sessions? After all, that's primarily how they're being graded in their classes!). The tutor, on the other hand, is primarily interested in improving the student as a *writer*, with less of an emphasis on the *writing*, as Stephen North told us a while back. Yes, it's that editor versus tutor contrast again.

Consider the writer's perspective. If the main goal of a session were to improve his paper, then his expectations for what you might do as tutor would be to make the corrections. After all, you're the writing "expert," and the end result would be much better if he were able to have you don your scrubs and perform a quick surgery on his ailing prose. However, as we have stressed up to this point, writing centers are not about editing. We are about teaching and maintaining a much larger view than correcting the immediate paper; our goals for sessions are to help the writer learn the skills needed to improve not just this paper but subsequent papers. So, do our long-term, process-oriented goals clash with writers' short-term, product-oriented goals? At times, yes, and one of your frequent tasks as a tutor will be to teach writers just what the writing center does and why a long-term view makes sense.

One important word about goals, however: It won't always be entirely clear what a writer's goals are, and you will need to work toward clarification. Consider the following list of actual requests writers issued at the start of sessions, often in response to the tutor's questions, "What can I help you with?" or "Why don't you tell me what you're working on?":

> "Well, I'm doing this paper on the construction of the pyramids for my archeology class, and basically I wrote it, and I guess my grammar and my word structure is not good enough. So I need a proofreader, and they advised me to come [here]."
>
> "If you could check the grammar?"
>
> "Basically, [focus on] the usage of words or idioms. Also, I have difficulty using the definite article 'the,' also some other articles, 'a' or 'the.'"
>
> "Well, just go through it, and, I mean, for punctuation. You don't have to correct it; just point out whether it's, like, punctuation mistakes but mainly both grammatical and sentence structure."
>
> "Look for grammar and misspellings, but see if you understand what I'm trying to say."
>
> "I want to know about the overall organization and maybe some expressions that I may not have used correctly in this paper."
>
> "I want to see what flows"
>
> "I wanted to see what you think."

"One of the things that I'm having a problem with is writing a book review; I've never really done a book review. I've also been under some personal issues I've been dealing with and trying to write this at the same time. I'm concerned about just the overall clarity and construction…and also if there happens to be grammatic stuff going on."

"I don't know how this works, so you should tell me how it works and then I'll just follow your lead because I've never been here before."

What would your reply be to these varied requests? After all, writers don't necessarily know the vocabulary of tutoring, and a "grammar check" request might mean a host of agenda items. Our point here is for you to be aware of the goals you and writers bring to tutoring sessions, to think about where the expectations for those goals might come from, and to scrutinize the language used to express those goals.

TAKING RESPONSIBILITY

Whatever your goals might be for a session, you have some expectations for what your responsibilities are to achieve those goals. In time, these expectations will come from study and practice of the art of tutoring writing, but before you're able to have those experiences, your expectations might be informed by factors you're not even quite aware of. We discussed cultural issues previously, and in the next section we present the powerful influence of your learning experiences. One factor related to both of these influences has to do with your perception of the relationship between tutors and writers. Who should be in "control" of the agenda? Who should be asking the questions? Who should control the "flow" of the session and be attentive to time and topic? Your answers to these questions all come from some source, some expectation for who should do what in a tutoring session. Literacy theorist James Gee and his colleagues believe that face-to-face interactions such as tutoring can be controlled by the participants' "ideologies" or "largely unconscious values and viewpoints within social activities that have implications for the distribution of power" (238). Being "largely unconscious," these ideologies are rarely critiqued, but instead many of us just express certain beliefs as the "right" way to do things. In tutoring, your attitudes toward the distribution of power will have a great influence on what occurs in your sessions.

Perhaps the clearest manifestation of power relationships in a session are your beliefs about your responsibilities and those of the writer you'll work with. Below is a list of responses to the question, "In a tutoring session, what are the responsibilities of tutors and writers?" generated by workshop

participants at the 13th annual meeting of the Northeast Writing Centers Association in Providence, RI. As you read these lists, consider not only which
you agree with, but more important, why.

Responsibilities of Tutors	Responsibilities of Writers
• Facilitate task • Be flexible • Set priorities • Be honest, yet diplomatic • Be respectful • Place equal importance on interpersonal skills and English knowledge • Find something positive • Serve as a model for approaching the task • Help writers enter disciplinary conversation • Create an alliance • Be on time • Negotiate responsibilities • Shift ownership of task to the writer • Listen well • Explain writing center mission • Understand the assignment • Help writer articulate goals	• Bring assignment, text, etc. • Bring motivation and openness • Be active, ask questions • Complete assignment and retain autonomy • Be respectful • Transfer knowledge across tasks and disciplines • Have realistic goals • Revisit work/follow up • Remain receptive to criticism while engaging in argumentative discourse • Bring specific goals • Create an alliance • Be on time • Be open to new discoveries

Workshop participants were primarily writing center directors and peer tutors. If students who use the writing center had been responding, do you think
the answers would have been different? Also, consider that many of these
items are open to interpretation. For instance, your interpretation of a "realistic
goal" might be different from the writer's. And those interpretations (or expectations) are again based upon your experiences, your notions of the ideal
relationship between tutors and writers, and a host of other factors.

A March 8, 1996, posting to the Internet discussion list WCenter, read by
more than 350 writing center directors and tutors, provides another example
for potentially mismatched expectations about responsibilities. Janet Mittendorf proposed the following definition of the "effective" tutor:

> *The effective writing tutor knows how to spot and help improve the most
> important problems in a written piece, how to keep the conference focused
> and productive, how to support the tutee's efforts while indicating areas*

ripe for improvement in the writing, and how to quickly forge a strong, pro-
fessional bond with tutees in order to motivate long-term improvements in
their writing processes.

At first reading, you'll probably find much of this description quite reasonable. But upon closer examination, consider how several of these items could
be quite different, depending upon one's perspective (and expectations). On
one level there would be difficulty in agreeing upon the "most important
problems in a written piece," in imagining what a "focused and productive"
conference would look like, and in describing abstract qualities such as
"support" and a "professional bond." On another level, embedded in this
definition are expectations for what each of these abstract characteristics
might be and expectations for the goals and responsibilities tutors should
adhere to in order to achieve this "effectiveness."

So have we hopelessly complicated tutoring at this point? We hope not.
Instead, we want you to give careful thought to why you feel as you do
about what writers and tutors should or should not do. Being reflective is
the key here. But before we end, we need to add one more major influence
on the expectations you'll bring to tutoring writing.

THE INFLUENCE OF TEACHERS

Consider for a moment who your most influential teachers have been or those
particularly powerful teaching/learning scenes that are etched in your memory (and those can be positive and negative). When it comes to writing, we
often remember teachers who encouraged us that we had something to say or
demanded clearer and clearer prose or who filled our drafts with red ink.

Now think about how you would go about helping someone else learn
to write—the advice you would give, the style of feedback, the strategies
you'd endorse. In the chapter on the writing process, we cautioned against
simply applying what works for you to another's situation. In the same way,
we want to caution applying (or immediately avoiding) those teaching and
learning experiences that you see so clearly in your mind's eye. Here's how
Shantel, a student at Marquette, described how her views of tutoring writing
were formed:

> I guess I have viewed tutoring in terms of power, that is, the tutor being
> the authority figure while the tutee submissively sits back watching the
> red pen marks disfigure his/her creation. This scene always seems to
> take place in a room with an imposing gray desk cluttered with papers,
> and for some strange reason *my* paper would always be lost among that
> heap. I never thought of tutoring defined in the terms of my friend who
> lived next door to me freshmen year, nor did I really have a clue that the

writing center tutors would be figures of lesser authority than my high school English teacher—who just happened to be a retired naval officer.

For Shantel, tutoring originally meant teaching in an authoritative, all-controlling way; hence, the contrast between tutors and "teachers" (or at least stereotypes of teachers!).

We don't mean to cast cynical doubt upon your experiences—after all, they might have been very effective for you. However, to simply apply those techniques in a different context can often be a frustrating experience for you and for the writer. Instead, you need to reflect deeply upon what some of your more influential learning experiences have been, think about the many factors that surrounded your experience and determined success (or failure). Overall, you need to listen and observe in a tutoring session, and ask yourself why you're acting in certain ways and where your actions are coming from.

In the same way, the writers with whom you'll work will have expectations for how you should act, expectations that come from *their* influential learning experiences. You will need to counter these expectations, open up lines of communication, and try to understand why writers are positioning you in certain ways.

For an example of the influence of one's learning experiences on her tutoring and the need to develop both control and flexibility as a tutor, we now introduce you to Adria. A writing tutor and a graduate student in Applied Linguistics, Adria had been an undergraduate dual major in biology and English and also had worked as a peer tutor. As you'll see, Adria has calm control over the writing strategies she passes along and hopes to help writers develop that control as well; however, in terms of flexibility, Adria often dispenses the same strategy to each writer, without regard for the particulars of that writer's process, task, or context for writing. Adria's impulse is good; after all, her goals are to increase a writer's strategic repertoire. However, as you'll see, her technique needs to be refined; there are limits to handing out the same strategies for each writer you encounter.

In a series of interviews, Adria talked about the influence of her student experiences on what she does as a writing tutor: "Some of the most fabulous professors I've had...shaped the way I write papers still today and the way that I teach my students to write." While listening to an audiotape of one of her sessions, Adria described that what she does involves "the whole notion of being systematic and explaining how I do these things and pass[ing] them along. That's what my professors have done for me, so I'm trying to do it for the student now."

In tutoring sessions that Adria tape-recorded, her approach often involved dispensing strategies as "hints" and "tricks." Adria would diagnose a problem in the writer's text, tell the writer of a helpful "trick" to fix that problem, and then show the writer how to apply that technique. As she told one writer during a session: "I'll tell you, you've come to the right place. I am Miss Shortcut. If there is a shortcut to be had, I've got it because I like to make things nice and simple." In another session in which a writer was working on a summary of an article, Adria tells her, "Okay, what I'm going to try to do is give you a few really helpful hints to help you make this a lot easier. Don't think that writing a summary should be difficult for somebody, and if I give you these hints, maybe it will be easier to do." When a writer expresses trouble with keeping her tenses consistent, Adria says, "I have a really good clue for that, a nice little trick. I like to do everything in nice little tricks; it makes it nice and easy."

For organizing ideas, Adria often prescribes using "glossing" or margin notes as a reading and revision strategy and writing an outline in order to organize ideas. For example, when giving a writer advice on composing an article summary, Adria tells her, "The best way to take care of this is as you go through each paragraph, jot down little notes in the margin, so when you go back, you don't have to reread the article again."

In the following example, the writer has drafted a memo recommending that a company purchase a piece of machinery. Adria models the margin-note strategy, summing up each paragraph of the writer's memo in a word or two in order to examine its structure. She elicits these summaries by rapidly questioning the writer on his chosen organizational pattern. As you read these transcript excerpts, keep in mind that they are written-down speech; thus, it might be best for you to read them aloud or, even better, read them with a partner, treating them as a script:

Adria: Okay, what did you mean by this part right here?

Writer: That's why the company should purchase the machine.

Adria: Okay, where do you tell the company to purchase the machine?

Writer: Up here.

Adria: Okay, where were you going to put the pros and cons?

Writer: In the middle.

Adria: Okay, why? Aren't they kind of scattered?

Writer: Yeah they are [writer laughs].

Adria: Okay, that's really what the problem is here. I think what you have to do is structure it a little bit more. So in this first part, what do you say?

Writer: Well, I said the company is not in good health.

Adria: Exactly. And you're very clear here. You have your numbers. You have your data and everything. So this is not in good health, we'll put that in the margin. [Adria writes] Okay? Now here, you're saying what? Your recommendation is to buy this machine.

Writer: Yeah.

Adria: Okay, "buy machine" here. And what are you saying down here? They should buy the machine.

Writer: Yeah, they should buy the machine. And in the middle, why they should buy the machine.

Adria: Okay, why they should buy the machine.

Writer: Well, the last one is the conclusion of something in the middle.

Adria: Okay. Where are you going to put the pros and cons? And here is not an option, right? Because you have "you should buy the machine," "why you should buy the machine," and "why you should buy the machine" as the conclusion.

Writer: After that.

Adria: Okay, exactly. So you need a whole new paragraph here.

This excerpt displays Adria's offering and modeling a specific strategy and reinforcing the use of that strategy. She asks for the writer's intentions by questioning and then evaluating the writer's memo with very specific comments ("Aren't they kind of scattered?" "So you need a whole new paragraph here."). Often these techniques will lead to Adria writing an outline or drawing a graphic that she will give writers at the end of the session.

In the next example, Adria is working with a different writer whose task was to summarize an article on funding mechanisms for brain-injured students. At the following point in the session, Adria sums up a series of her questions and the writer answers to discern the gist of the article:

Adria: So let's make up a little trick because this can get kind of confusing. [Adria writes on a separate piece of paper] So because there's no agreement, there is no definition. Because there is no definition, there is no money. And because there is no money, there is no help. So this is kind of what happens. They're trying to tell you, and there's a little bit of a discrepancy here because they're trying to tell you, "Well there's no help because there's no definition," and in reality there's no help because there's no money. And there's no money because there's no definition. So they're leaving that step out. Does that make sense?

Writer: Yeah.

Adria: Because this is all stuff you've told me; I'm just laying it all out for you. Okay, so you want to talk about this whole argument probably. "Well this is a big problem. There is no help. The reason there is no help is because…" Does this make sense?

Writer: Mmm, hmm.

Adria: Okay, I'm just recapping everything that you've told me, and I'm just organizing it.

In this exchange Adria plays a directive role in producing a "coherent" narrative for the writer ("So let's make up a little trick because this can get kind of confusing.") while phrasing the results as a joint effort ("I'm just recapping everything that you've told me, and I'm just organizing it.") and frequently checking the writer's understanding ("Does this make sense?").

In many ways, Adria's approach seems quite effective. After all, we described in Chapters 2 and 3 many strategies you can use at various points in a session. Doesn't it make sense to pass those strategies along to writers? Isn't increasing a writer's strategic repertoire aligned with the goal of focusing on her as a *writer*?

Well, yes and no. Writing center theorist Andrea Lunsford describes a model of the "Writing Center as Storehouse" which "operates as information stations or storehouses, prescribing and handing out skills and strategies to individual learners" (4). Lunsford is critical of this approach because it sets writers up as autonomous units with similar needs and ignores the collaborative nature of learning. The social nature and complexity of learning to write confound the goal of dispensing "hints and tricks."

On a more obvious level, the one-size-fits-all nature of these strategies was not readily accepted by all writers. In an interview with the writer in the excerpt about funding for brain-injured students, she commented upon the usefulness of one strategy Adria endorsed. The purpose of this strategy was to overcome getting "stuck" while writing by saying, "Wait a minute. I'm stuck. How would I tell this to Adria? What would I say to her?" This writer noted that "I think it was easier said than done.… easier for her to say to me, 'Oh, do it like that.' It doesn't always work like that.… It's more, it's not as easy, you can't just tell someone and write down what you want to tell them." She wondered if using "the same things per person" might not always work since "you don't know the people."

So is Adria a horrible tutor, one who will besmirch the reputation of the writing center? Certainly not, and we don't mean to "bash" her here. Adria is a resourceful tutor, one who has expertise into many facets of the tutoring process. However, she has very explicit, if not rigid, ideas of what her goals and responsibilities are in a session, and those ideas stem from how she feels she best learned to write. In many instances, writers gratefully appreciate being shown strategies that they can use on their own. In other instances, however, Adria's lack of flexibility won't be as effective. Adria needs to strike a balance and uncover the writer's needs more fully.

Our point for you here is to reflect upon the ways of tutoring that feel "right." Where do they come from? How much flows from what worked for you as a writer? Rather than merely transmit strategies or even enact practices that you've seen work in other sessions (whether that means asking questions or having the writer read aloud or any other strategy), the important thing is to approach a session with a curious and open mind and, once again, to develop control of the strategies that you might offer writers and the flexibility to know what's working in a session and what adjustments you need to make. What you'll often find to be your most important resource isn't what you can tell writers, but instead what you do instead of talking. In other words, by listening and observing, by looking at body language and uncovering what the writer is doing and why, you can succeed in any tutoring session.

We'd like you to give careful thought to the role your expectations are playing in what's happening or about to happen. Whether that means negotiating the "rules" of communication or holding in check the endorsement of an infallible strategy, as an effective tutor you'll need to be a careful observer and a thoughtful communicator. We never said that tutoring would be easy, but in its difficulty and complexity lie great rewards and thought-provoking experiences.

5

OBSERVING IN THE WRITING CENTER

We both learn a great deal from observing our tutors. We're always picking up new, better strategies we wouldn't have thought of on our own, and we're able to admire the way our tutors function in different circumstances. In the same way, tutors—new and experienced—learn from observing one another. Thus, the contrast between "novice" and "expert" is blurred as the writing center becomes a place of collaborative learning, not just for writers, but for the staff as well.

In this chapter, we want to introduce you to the essentials of observation. In an activity as interactive as tutoring, it might not be altogether obvious just how important effective observing can be. Whether you are observing the sessions of an experienced tutor as you try to learn from the model of others or whether you're observing the behaviors a writer displays in your own sessions, we think that observing well is one of the best ways you'll develop as a tutor.

Here's what Caroline Goyette, a peer tutor at Marquette, wrote about the importance of her observation experiences:

> The tutoring sessions which I have observed to date have been quite different from one another in terms of focus, goals, and approach. From them, I believe I have learned much about the manner in which the tutoring methods espoused here may be applied to a wide variety of tutoring needs, as well as the ability of the individual tutor to manipulate these methods to form his/her own unique and effective tutoring style. Above all, however, my observation experience has given me the

confidence to tutor by showing me that there is no trick, no secret method or cryptic agenda to which every tutor must adhere.

In what follows, we first establish some of the essentials to keep in mind when observing the tutoring sessions of another or the behaviors of writers when participating in your own. We'll also give you some advice about how to get the most out of it, and we'll tell you how we have our tutor trainees learn to observe. Finally, we'll take you through a brief excerpt from an actual tutorial and point out some observations that will help you begin to make sense of the sessions you will see.

GET PERMISSION

First, it's really important to have the cooperation of the director or person who runs your writing center. Let him or her know what you want to do and why, if a process of observation isn't already in place. It's going to be important that both the tutor *and the writer* feel comfortable being observed, too. At Marquette, we have an understanding with our experienced tutors that if it's all right with the writer, they could be observed at any session. If they don't feel comfortable with this, they can tell us, and we make sure our trainees know which tutors they can observe and which ones aren't ready for observation yet. To observe a session at Marquette, all one needs to do is check the schedule (see the example schedule page at the end of this chapter), find a time when someone is working with a writer, and pencil his or her name in as an observer. If possible, they schedule a session with the tutor immediately afterwards so they can discuss what they saw. This means they'd be signing up for two time slots, one with a writer present, and one for just them and the tutor. We recommend one observer to a session to keep writers from feeling overwhelmed.

OBSERVE SEVERAL SESSIONS

Observe as many different tutors as your training program allows, and observe different sessions with the same tutors. You'll see a very rich range of tutoring strategies, and you'll see an individual tutor vary his style or approach depending on the writer he gets and the kind of session they have (brainstorming or revising, for example). You'll also see differences based on how well the tutor knows the writer, and how many sessions they've had together. A tutor working for a third session with the same writer might just dispense with the early talk and jump right into the session, eager to see the draft. You'll see differences in the comfort level, too, and maybe in levels of formality with these repeat visits.

BE ON TIME!

Be sure to show up early for your observation. You don't want to interrupt after the session has started, and observing the tutor from the very start of the session is a very important part of what you'll get out of the observation. Either you or the tutor will ask the writer if he or she minds being observed, and if it's OK, then you're set.

RECORD YOUR OBSERVATIONS

Be sure to bring paper and a pencil or pen to take notes. As you observe, you won't get everything written down, but take as many notes as you can. The trainees at Marquette have a log they keep of the sessions they observe and conduct (see the example log at the end of this chapter). This log is intended to provide material for reflective papers the trainees write at various times during the semester, but it's also useful for them to see the way they develop both as observers and as tutors.

BE OPEN-MINDED

Consider these scenarios: Does a writer slumping in her chair mean she's bored? Does a writer rapidly reading from his text, barely allowing the tutor to understand or keep up, indicate he's not crazy about coming to the writing center? Does a writer nodding vigorously to everything the tutor says and indicating with "yes" and "aha" mean that she completely agrees?

Certainly these conclusions for the observed behaviors could be true. But alternative explanations could be true as well. Perhaps the slumping writer had a lousy night's sleep? Perhaps the rapid reader just has little practice with reading aloud? And perhaps the eager nodder is thinking about her plans for the upcoming weekend and is simply trying to have the tutor do all the talking!

The bottom line here is that what you observe in a tutoring session can have multiple meanings. That means not only that you have to reserve judgment of what you see until you have as much information as possible (or not to make judgments if you can help it), but that you have to increase your powers of observation, to notice the subtle clues of behavior that you might ordinarily have missed.

We encourage our tutor trainees to stay as objective as possible, recording what they see. For instance, you may find yourself formulating different questions for the writer, questions that would take the session in a different direction than the questions you hear the tutor asking. Relax about this. There are many ways to take a session, all of which will help the writer improve. So your role is not to evaluate the tutor, but to look for good qualities you can adopt.

It might be a good idea to jot some of your questions down, however. You never know when a tutor might turn to you and ask if you want to participate.

DISCUSS THE SESSION

With a little luck, you'll have a chance to talk the session over with the tutor. Whether you do or not, we think it's important that you have a chance to talk it over with someone. Usually you'll feel very comfortable, because you'll be full of praise for what went on. It's good to talk with someone else who has also been observing sessions, so talking to another trainee is a very good idea. If you have a training class or group that meets, that's another good place to discuss your observation.

REFLECT ON THE SESSION

How, then, can you make sense of what you saw? As you look back at your notes, respond to as many of the following reflective/analytical questions as you can.

- How did the tutor make the writer feel welcome?
- What body language did she use? Did she smile? Make small talk as they got started?
- What questions did the tutor ask about the assignment or paper?
- Were there additional questions you'd have asked?
- How did the tutor use the space available to make the writer feel comfortable?
- Was the tutor a good listener? How could you tell?
- Who did most of the talking?
- Did the tutor seem to respect the writer's work? How did she communicate this?
- Did the tutor address the questions the writer came with?
- If the tutor had a different agenda from the writer, how did she negotiate that?
- Did the writer respond well to the tutor's style? Why do you think so? Or think not?
- What kinds of questions did the tutor ask about the project?
- How do you think the writer responded to those questions?
- How did the tutor make known the responsibilities of tutor and writer in the session? What did she say or do?
- How would you describe the role of the tutor: editor, coach, authority figure, peer?

- If the tutor needed to change the subject, or get the session back on track, how did she do that?
- How did the tutor end the session?
- Did you feel that the writer knew what she would do next to revise?
- Did the tutor ask her to return?

As you reflect upon what you observed, trust your sense of the session. Did it seem positive? What did the writer seem to get out of the session? Did he or she feel pleased at the end? Did his or her attitude change toward the paper? How could you tell? Was the paper the main subject of the session, or did the session primarily focus on the writer's composing strategies? Most important, what did you get out of the session? What new things did you learn, or what techniques did you spot?

WRITE UP YOUR OBSERVATIONS

As we have mentioned, your observations and reflections can become the source for a reflective essay, a powerful way of using writing to understand how you're developing as a tutor. What follows is one tutor's account of observations, taken from a reflective paper required for the peer tutoring course at Marquette:

> My jaw dropped. Attending my English 192 class for the first time, I was already contemplating my withdrawal from this class. Paula had just informed us that 20 hours of tutoring and observation in the writing center was required to pass the course. This writing center business was most unexpected. Being a very conscientious student, I had registered for English 192 without any idea what it was about. I knew it was a writing class, which is what I required for graduation. Normally, the unknown is a frightening spectre; however, this time I saw a rare opportunity to seek truth in a foreign environment. Little did I realize I would learn a great deal about helping others, about myself, and the power of a chicken sandwich.
>
> I was eager, if a bit apprehensive, to begin observing tutoring sessions in progress. I had never felt the need to spend any time at the writing center prior to this. Due to a combination of shyness, decent writing skills, and what my father would call "bull-headedness," I could never bring myself to ask for help on a paper. Fortunately, the tutors, whom I had encountered at the first writing center staff meeting, seemed friendly and helpful. Naturally, I didn't trust them.
>
> My first session was spent in observation of Crystal, who was working with a female first-year student on a reflective essay about a time

when she changed her mind about something. It was their second session together. They seemed to have a good rapport. Even I felt comfortable, despite the pervasive feeling that I was guilty of a kind of academic voyeurism. The student was very concerned about word choice and "flow." At the tutor's request, the student read her paper aloud. It was about the moment she realized she would not qualify for state in track as a senior in high school. Crystal asked leading questions, forcing the student to think for herself. I felt this was very positive, and began to see where Crystal was heading. Eventually, the student learned what to look for, and was catching problematic phrases before she read them. She revised her descriptions as well, making them more vivid, eye-catching. In this case, the tutor not only helped the student revise a paper, but indirectly taught her to see her paper from a third-person perspective. Impressed, I left the writing center with a renewed hope for mankind, or something like that.

As I walked to my car, I reflected on what I had just witnessed. I began to mentally reenact the session, only with myself as the tutor. Full of confidence, I felt as if there were some things that I would have suggested to make the student's paper greater still. Delusional visions of an "ideal text" filled my head. Deliciously assembled articulations spilled from my brain like something of a spillable consistency. The paper was mine to manipulate, to shape into my own monster (insert evil laughter here).

"Growwwwl," said my stomach, objecting to my ignorance of standard breakfast protocol. It was the occasion of my second observation, and I was hungry for a chicken sandwich. Sarah was seeing a male physics student working on his dissertation. His primary concern was grammar and punctuation. Sarah obligingly pored over each phrase with him, reading silently as the student read aloud. He obviously felt very comfortable with Sarah, as he felt no remorse in asking her opinions on each (real or imagined) transgression he stumbled upon. Like Crystal, Sarah was doing a superior job, making the student feel at home while maintaining a professional distance. I dutifully took notes despite my emaciated state and the haunting image of a chicken sandwich impressed onto my brain. Initially I had felt intimidated about the stature of the assignment at hand. However, as he read, I found that the dissertation actually made sense to me, and I regained my tutorial egotism. Sarah, in a not so subtle attempt to make me feel more useful, asked my opinion on three or four occasions. This unleashed the writer within, determined to create order out of chaos, to impose truth where truth was not necessarily wanted or needed.

As the session wound down and Sarah was taking care of the paper work, I began to compose on the topic of my hunger, just for sport. More precisely, I wove a tapestry of unbridled and powerful prose about the philosophical, aesthetic, and practical importance of the chicken sandwich. Chicken sandwich as the path to nirvana. Chicken sandwich as neo-realist art. Chicken sandwich as paperweight (I had just read Nancy Sommers).[1] Obviously, the hunger was starting to affect my brain. I was so ready for a chicken sandwich at the time, and when I finally got one, it would be the best I ever had. It would have to wait until tomorrow, as I was out of money.

Next, I met with Joe, only this time it was to have him tutor me. Since I scarcely had any real draft, we instead brainstormed on what I might write about regarding my tutoring experiences. It was then that Joe made a statement that has since defined my view of the writing center. "We are not here to write their papers for them. It's not ours, it's theirs, for better or worse, lumps and all. Not every paper is going to change the world."

He was right. I could not hope to guide each student into my view of an ideal text. The best I could hope for is to help them make the best of the paper that they bring in. As I sat down at Boston Market to enjoy my long anticipated chicken sandwich, it hit me. Sometimes, a paper is not going the be the Mona Lisa of English 01 papers. Likewise, sometimes a chicken sandwich is not going to be the Taj Mahal of chicken sandwiches. As I tasted my Holy Quail, I sighed. It was a little dry.

–Daniel Scherrer

Dan first observed Crystal, a graduate student, and then Sarah, a senior. Notice, though, that Sarah is tutoring a graduate student working on a dissertation. She doesn't have to be an expert in physics, though, to tell if his writing is clear and correct.

REFLECT AGAIN

After you've had some tutoring experience of your own, it's a good idea to look over these accounts of the sessions you observed. They will mean different things to you at different points in your training. It might be good for you to write up a narrative the way the tutors at Marquette do (though your stomach needn't always play a role in these essays), and send them to *The Writing Lab Newsletter* Tutor's Corner, or to the NWCA website, where tutor stories are published. These kinds of stories and observations help us all know more, not only about the training process, but about the tutoring process.

---

[1] Dan had just read "Between the Drafts" by Sommers.

EXAMPLES FOR OBSERVATION

To help you practice making sense of what you'll observe in "live" tutoring sessions, we include two transcript excerpts. Both come from the beginning of sessions. With the first, we'll supply some analysis, but we'll leave the second one for your comments and scrutiny. As you read these (and we recommend you read each aloud, preferably with a partner taking the second speaking role), picture the scene in your head. Use the reflective questions we posed earlier in this chapter to make sense of what you're "seeing."

In this first example, the writer has already told the tutor that she's writing a book review for her graduate education class. The transcript picks up from that point:

Tutor: How do you want to proceed? I'm wondering if I should have you read this to me; yeah, it's only four pages. Will you do that? And that way you can include the comments, or additions, or changes better than I would be able to.

Writer: Okay, personally I find this first paragraph, I know what I'm trying to say and I find this kind of awkward. Okay? And I don't know why.

Tutor: What are you trying to say? Before you read it to me, tell me what you're trying to say, then I can hear it.

Writer: Okay, well what I'd like to discuss is just the…I guess to bring the reader of this piece into the idea of my opinion of what Alphabet City, or the place where this book was going to happen, before I even got into the book. I had some biases.

Tutor: Interesting.

Writer: It's a preconceived thing. That's just sort of a way to talk about where this book is taking place. And then get into the book and so that's…

Tutor: So in a sense this is your response to the book? You want your reader to know where you started in your response to the book?

Writer: Okay.

Tutor: At what point you were? Is that correct?

Writer: Yeah, I never said it to anyone, I just started trying to write it. Yeah, I guess I'm just trying to set up what my impression was before I picked up the book.

Notice several things in this excerpt about what the tutor does. He asks the writer to read her text aloud, justifying that request ("And that way you can include the comments, or additions, or changes better than I would be able to.") by demonstrating that she's the "expert," she's the one in control of her paper and will need to be the one to revise. When the writer next expresses disdain for her first paragraph, the tutor asks her to clarify it for him before she reads anything. In that way he probes the clarity of her thoughts, discovering if it's her writing that's unclear or if her understanding of what she's read and trying to convey needs work. Also, notice that after the writer explains her first paragraph, the tutor rephrases her explanation in terms of "a reader" ("You want your reader to know where you started in your response to the book?"). By doing this, he conveys to the writer the need to think in terms of the rhetorical situation, particularly her purpose in her first paragraph and how she's trying to convey that purpose to her reader. Finally, note that the tutor doesn't simply announce his clarifying of the writer's intentions; he asks her to verify ("At what point you were? Is that correct?").

In these moves, the tutor establishes what his role is: to support the writer as *she* clarifies her meaning and to demonstrate how to think about her writing in rhetorical terms. He also establishes the writer's role to convey her interpretation of the book and for her to make "comments, additions, or changes." Now, consider that this excerpt took only a minute and 15 seconds! Certainly, much of the important work of your sessions will take place at the very beginning.

The next excerpt is for your practice observation. As you read and examine this passage (again, reading aloud if possible), think about the roles that tutor and writer play. What do they seem to convey to each other in terms of their goals and responsibilities? How can you tell? Once again, the following passage comes at the very beginning of the session. Note, too, that dialogue in all capital letters indicates the reading of a text aloud:

Tutor: Since you haven't been here before, could you please fill this out for me, and I'll read over your assignment while you're…

Writer: I think the first thing that I want…it's for art history. It's about the architectural, the Boston Public Library and the Museum of Fine Arts and I had problems with the first paper. He said to me that he knew that I had a good ideas but he couldn't understand them because they were not well written. So I want you to sort of…

Tutor: Look for those things?

Writer: Yes. Look for grammar and misspellings but to see if you understand what I'm trying to say.

Tutor: Okay. Fantastic. Do you have your assignment with you so that I can read what your professor asked for?

Writer: He didn't give us something written. It's just a paper on the additions of the Museum of Fine Arts and the Boston Public Library.

[silence while writer fills out forms]

Tutor: Okay. All set?

Writer: Yeah.

Tutor: How about you read through this out loud and I'll listen, and you might find things yourself as you read along that maybe aren't so clear, and then we can work as we go.

Writer: You read it already?

Tutor: No, I haven't read it already, but it just makes more sense for us to do it this way today.

Writer: Okay. Do you want me to read it?

Tutor: Out loud.

Writer: Out loud?

Tutor: Yeah.

Writer: Oh, okay.

Tutor: Sometimes when you hear things, you pick up, if something's difficult to understand or doesn't quite flow, you'll hear it. Your ears will recognize it before your eyes do sometimes.

Writer: Oh, wow, okay. AN ADDITION TO AN EXISTING CORPUS, IN THIS CASE A LIBRARY AND A MUSEUM, IS A VERY DIFFICULT TASK TO REALIZE FOR AN ARCHITECT. Could you tell me when I'm not saying the words the way I should?

GOOD OBSERVING = GOOD TUTORING

In a session that lasts from 30 to 60 minutes, you'll have plenty to watch for, plenty to record, and plenty to make sense of. It might be difficult at first, but learning to observe takes time and patience. We're convinced that good tutoring starts with good observing, and that as you gain experience, your powers of observation—and your ability to reflect upon what you observe—will become some of your greatest assets in your development as a writing tutor.

TUTOR & ROOM # *(pointing to Val 450)*

	Week Twelve		**Monday, November 16, 1998**		
	Kelly 467	Stacie 476	(Val 450)	Stewart 432	Crystal 472
9:00	Heather Schmidt *ANDY*	Angela Bohlke *BRAD*			
9:30	↓ 332-8864	↓ 456-5665			
10:00	Shane Ethan *ANDY*	Gabriel Diques 229-4331 *BRAD*	Letitia Gomez *SARA*		
10:30	↓ 933-8910	Brenda Cardenas	↓ 229-3992		
11:00	Craig Woytal *KRISTINA*	↓ 261-3001			
11:30	↓ 962-2516	Brad			
12:00					Erica Gumm *ROBYN*
12:30					↓ 933-3339
1:00				Lee Kennedy *SHANTEL*	Sheri
1:30				332-5933	
2:00				Robert Barker *SHANTEL*	
2:30				592-5993	
3:00					
3:30					
4:00			Emma Baker *ADELE*		
4:30			961-4553		

WRITER & PHONE # *(pointing to Emma Baker / 961-4553)*

OBSERVER *(pointing to ADELE)*

English 192 Writing Center Tutoring Log

Name __Adele Smith__

Please draw a line across the page after each session.

Date	Time In	Out	Description of session	Supervisor's Initials
9-20	6:30	7:40	Read Ben's paper over on e-mail. He had a lot of really great ideas, but lacked some focus. My main concern was that he did not clearly explain his thesis. The paper was going in a bunch of different directions, it seemed. I asked a number of questions about order & expansion of ideas.	AS
9/23	1:00	1:35	I observed w/ Stewart, tutoring a freshman who had the assignment of writing about a transition & how he changed his view of something significant. Throughout the session Stewart asked the tutee questions, most of which he did not answer, but rather nodded his head & said "Yeah, that's a good idea, that will work." Both Stewart & I attempted to ask leading questions, and a few times we had to say "Will you TELL me?" This led to a sort of directive approach by the tutor, but I do think that the tutee walked out with more ideas and he agreed that the session was very helpful.	EW
10/7	10:00	11:00	Andy & Val's session was so awesome. Andy came in with a pretty rough draft - something he had typed very late the night before, but he had some really great ideas - they just needed a lot of explaining. Val asked a bunch of "what do you mean by that" questions. This really got Andy talking about his paper. It was totally textbook and Andy said it helped out a ton. It helped me out a ton too, because I got to see how Andy really improved his thoughtfulness by the end of the session.	VM
10/0	2:00	3:00	This was my session for the reflective essay - and the first time I have gone to the writing center to be tutored. (I loved it - I'm definitely going back with other papers). This was a helpful session because Stewart and I were able to clear up some concerns I had about the explanation of my ideas in my paper. When I write reflectives or analyses, it is easy to confuse the reader (because I know what I am talking about, and I sometimes forget to explain it clearly). It also helped for us to just talk about tutoring because it gave me some good ideas that I might of otherwise looked over.	EW

6

THE MOCK TUTORIAL

We're calling this chapter "The Mock Tutorial," but rather than think of the contrast of mock versus real, think of what we'll describe as practice. You'll get tutored—and you'll tutor someone else—on a piece of real writing, and something really good can come out of this practice.

There are many reasons why we really like to use this exercise in our training, including:

- As the tutor, you'll get to listen to a text being read aloud, and then get to try out note-taking.
- As the tutor, you'll also get to formulate questions about the text you hear.
- As the writer, you'll get tutored on work you really wrote, and you'll even enjoy that process.
- As the writer, you'll get to see how different it is reading aloud and getting some, perhaps, unexpected feedback on your work.
- As the observer, you'll get to help the tutor by affirming what she's doing well, and you'll also get practice observing and with taking notes on that process.

There are all kinds of ways you can take part in a mock tutorial. You could read someone else's paper and act out the role of the writer, but we think that the scenario we describe below works best. Plan to work in groups of three. They don't all have to be trainees, if other trainees aren't available, but all trainees would be best. However, two experienced tutors and one trainee would work just fine.

There are three roles you'll play in this triad: the writer, the tutor, and the observer. The writer brings a piece of his own writing, a paper you've handed in and like a lot, one you're working on, or an old one you'd genu-inely like to revise. It will help if you're really open-minded about the ques-tions and comments the tutor makes about your paper. You could really learn a lot about your own writing from this.

The tutor will conduct this as if it were a real session, asking names, get-ting acquainted, asking about the assignment, asking what the writer likes about it and what he wants to work on. The writer reads the paper as if this were a real session, and the tutor takes notes and then asks questions of the writer and gives feedback.

Meanwhile, the observer is taking notes on what is going on in the ses-sion, and after it's over will answer the questions

- What happened?
- What did you see?
- What did the writer get out of the session?
- What was good about the session?"

Allow at least a half hour for the whole tutorial: a few minutes for precon-ference talk and questions about the assignment, paper, and so forth; about seven minutes to read the paper aloud (assuming it's about five pages); a few minutes for the tutor to gather her thoughts, about ten minutes of good questions; and then about five to ten minutes for the observer to comment. If a class of tutors can break into groups and do this, then it's good to com-pare notes at the end and see what came out of it for the entire class.

A SAMPLE SESSION

In a mock tutorial session, Adele agreed to read a paper she'd written in her first year composition class. It was a paper she wasn't quite satisfied with, but one that had earned a good grade, and she still had some unresolved feelings about it, felt it should have been better, but the teacher's comments didn't help her to see how. You might want to read this paper aloud and for-mulate your own questions about it; then read the dialogue below that Adele had with Aesha, who agreed to be the tutor. After some introductory talk and a description of the assignment (a paper written to other students trying to convince them of something), Adele read:

On November 3rd I attended the men's basketball game. On November 9th, yet another. On November 7th, a girl's basketball game. Did anyone want to join me? Because when I asked people if they went to the game, I got a lot of "Well, no. I had a lot to do." Hey, I had a lot to do too! The funny thing is that most of the people I had asked to go to the game were also Fanatic Club members. I say that if you are going to spend that much money on season tickets, you might as well attend the games. The T-shirts you get aren't all that great, so what motivated these students to purchase tickets? Who knows! But I do know that this season is bringing another display of Marquette's lack of school spirit.

What is so darn important about school spirit, you ask? Let's concentrate on athletics. Marquette is a Division 1 school, our men's basketball team is the defending Conference-USA Champion, our women's track members are the defending Conference-USA Champions, our men's soccer team is going to the finals, our women's soccer team finished their home season undefeated and second in the C-USA Conference. I'd say we have a pretty strong athletic program here at Marquette. So what is stopping you from displaying some enthusiasm about it? You can't do homework all the time. And even if you do, there needs to be a balance in your life between recreation and studying. Take a break! The games are only a couple hours long. And trust me—you will certainly be refreshed when the game is over.

So are we just scared to be enthusiastic? I don't think we are, at least we shouldn't be. If you love something enough to be a part of it, as you are of Marquette, then show it! There must be some reason you chose this school. Show people how proud you are to be a Golden Eagle. Attend a basketball game or two, or ten if you want to. (Support your soccer teams, too. The Fall Festival had a pathetic attendance.) And since you're there, you might as well cheer for your team. And don't just cheer at the Cincinnati or Louisville games. I'm pretty sure that the players would like to hear some screaming at all of their games. Losing against Dayton can be just as detrimental to their season as losing against Cincinnati.

Going to games also gives you a great opportunity to get involved socially by meeting people other than those in your classes or at parties. Most of the students sit in the same section, so all of your friends are going to be right there with you. The games provide a chance for you to let loose, scream a little, and just to have a great time.

I don't know if you all watched or went to the University of Wisconsin–Madison game, but you could have learned a valuable lesson on school spirit from them. They actually stood up and cheered when their team scored, and even more so when their team was down. They seemed to be having so much fun. For a second I almost wanted to go over and sit with them just because our own student section was so downbeat. But I am dedicated to Marquette, and to creating a spirit like so many other colleges have.

I need your help though. It takes more than just twenty people at the games. Do you laugh at the schools that get all dressed up and paint their faces, and make signs for games? Call it stupid? I call it spirit. And that is what we need. We are a university. Have you ever really looked at the word "university"? Do you see the word *unity* in there somewhere? Do you see how we should support our fellow students, and our entire school to defend our unity?

So get up and say for once "this reading can wait." None of us can study all the time, and if you really do, then take a break! Go out and do something important to you and to your university. Offer the encouragement to our students that the Marquette Jesuit tradition is "famous" for. Don't be the student that walks away from college having only studied and partied. You are only in college for a few short years, but if you get involved, you become a part of your university, making memories and leaving your mark forever.

Aesha asked Adele: What were your main reasons in support of going to the games?

Adele: We should be willing to support our sports program because we have really good teams. Going to games is a way to get involved. We should have more team spirit.

Aesha: How did you support your claims?

Adele: I felt I was really critical of other students and of our school. Does it sound too critical of the people I was trying to persuade?

Aesha: If you were reading it, would you be offended? (Lots of laughing)

Adele: I'd really like to change the tone. It's too much like a slap in the face. I think I did too much accusing. I'd like to suggest a course of action instead.

Aesha asked a series of questions:
- "What do you think is the problem? Why don't people go to the games?"
- "How can you persuade people who don't want to go to attend?"
- "What makes *you* want to go?"
- "What course of action would you want to propose?"
- "What are other people's views on the subject?"

These questions led Adele to think of a section she could have added to the paper to suggest ways to get students more interested in showing school spirit by attending games. She also noted that she hadn't included any opposition in her paper, something she would add if she revised it. By the end of the tutorial, Adele had a very good sense of how she would revise the paper and how she would improve it.

THE OBSERVATION

If you were the observer, what would you point out? During this mock tutorial session, Sheri was the observer. She noted that Aesha was not condescending and seemed interested, that she listened and smiled during the discussion. She liked the way Aesha let Adele say what she really thought; she felt the good questions allowed that to happen. She complimented Aesha on the way she let the writer come up with the answers.

Reflections on the Mock Tutorial:

After we finished the mock tutorials, we discussed the process over in class. Then we asked the trainees to discuss it in our electronic journal. Here were some responses.

> The mock tutorial was an excellent experience for me. When I was working with Angela I realized my…tendency to, well…shred. I had been thinking about those directive tendencies and wondering how I'd overcome them. It was all that was going through my head as I addressed an 001 class at 8 am today. There I was saying, "Yeah, Yeah, come to the writing center where we're all so supportive and helpful," and I was feeling a tiny bit bad about the whole thing. Anyway, 9:00 rolled around and I had the chance to mock-tutor Shantel. I think the whole thing went much better. (Can you back me up on that, Shantel? Please?!)
>
> One thing I have found in the mock tutorial, though, is that I really want to see the paper as it's read. This is mostly because I'd like to make notes near the positive and negative aspects of the paper. That way we could avoid all of the awkward moments of, "ooh, wait, you had something about…wait…this note doesn't make sense, yeah, I can't read my own writing, ummmmmmmmmmmmm…well, never mind."
>
> I don't know if it's okay to make a copy. Is it, Paula? Well, if it's not protocol, I guess I'll just have to get quicker and neater with the pen.
>
> –Susan

Most new tutors share Susan's concern about being able to listen well enough to take good notes and come up with good questions at the same time. And they worry about their history of "shredding." You'll get lots of practice at listening and formulating questions when you start observing others, and if you feel you need even more, ask someone to read you the sample papers you'll find in Chapter 7.

Like those of you who have responded already, I also have found the mock tutorials to be a big help. I can hear about something in class and read about it in a textbook, but it usually doesn't click for me until I have to apply it myself.

I have to admit that I was a little nervous about playing the tutor. I wasn't sure if I would be able to do it. I had this horrible vision of me listening to the student read her paper and then either having nothing to say or having so much to say that I had no idea where to start. I was afraid of being utterly clueless. Actually doing a tutorial in class has helped me to see that I'm a lot better at it than I thought I would be. Not that I'm perfect by any means, but at least I know that I won't fall flat on my face! I think that our exercises in class have done a lot to boost my confidence level.

Also, during my tutorial with Kristina I learned that listening, being patient, and being able to ask good questions are more important than "having all the answers" about a particular subject. I knew nothing about what she was writing about—an autobiographical essay on her life for grad school—but by asking broad questions on her experiences, I think I was able to help her brainstorm about where to go next with her paper. As far as patience goes, I learned that sometimes you need to be comfortable with silence while the student thinks about what she would like to say next. It was tempting for me to jump in at one point, but I needed to let her think before she responded to a question I had asked.

–Sara

We think that there are so many good questions to ask a writer that you'll never come up empty. It's always a good idea to ask the writer, "Now that you've read the paper, what do you want to do with it to revise?" That gives you a breather while the writer gets warmed up talking about revision.

We also believe in the power of silence. It's surprising to notice how little time some professors give students to reply to questions in class before they give out the "right" answer. But sometimes it takes a minute to process a good question and think of a good answer, so give the writer a minute and don't consider all silences awkward.

Hey All. This is Andy, and I would like to say that, like everyone else, I find these mock tutorials enlightening. They have given me an idea of what the tutoring process will be like and such without being in the pressure-packed environs of the writing center. Sara's comment about the importance of "being able to ask good questions" really rang true (I hate that phrase but can't think of anything better now) for me. When I was tutoring people I found if I asked them open-ended questions, they had a lot to say about what they wrote and that gave me ideas for further questions to ask them. I like following the questions or concerns the writer has about the paper because these need to be cleared up to give a writer confidence in his/her work and a lot of times they're more observant than I am—they see things that I didn't. I think part of that is that they have had more time with their paper, so they have had more time to meditate on details and such. Also, though, Paula reminded me, when she did a little mock tutoring, to tutor the paper as a whole. She thought something was lacking from the main point of a paper our group was working on, and she brought that up to the writer. However, she did it tactfully and in a conversational way, and the writer agreed with what she had to say. It felt more like Paula was drawing the more complex ideas out of the writer, more than telling the writer to make her ideas more complex. The writer did most of the talking. I guess it goes back to asking good questions, maybe also making good conversation. Maybe its a bit of a Zen thing. Other than that, I've learned from tutoring that I'm a slow note taker, so I've gotten a bunch of books on tape from the library and am practicing my shorthand. My goal is to write Moby Dick in shorthand in under ten hours, with margin comments on things that are good, and what needs improvement.

–Andy

Andy's observation that new questions arise as the writer talks about the paper is a good one. You don't have to have a whole session's worth of questions. A few good ones at the beginning will get the ball rolling well.

Well, I have to agree with everybody in the sense that these mock tutorials help out a lot. The best part is that I got to see all sides of the tutorial. From the pressure of being a tutor, to the pressure of being a tutee, I was able to see the whole picture. I still feel that probably the worst part of the tutoring process is the "awkward silence" that can occur when someone is thinking of changes to make. I hate awkward silence. Anyway, I really feel that these whole mock tutorials are a big help in getting a firm grasp on what it is we will be attempting this semester. I realize that I am not here to help a student create the world's greatest paper and then be praised in their acceptance speech for every award that they receive. It really just dawned on me today that the tutor's job is just to unlock what it is the writer wants to say. Not what the tutor wants the writer to say.

–Paul

Right now I am in the basement of the library which is pretty creepy because I've never been down here before. Anyway, I thought the mock tutorials were a tremendous help. Before we started the tutorials, I thought I had the tutoring thing down-pat: I take a few notes, try not to give my opinion, and use directive questioning. However, after my first time tutoring, I realized I had no reason to be that confident. I learned that not giving your own opinion is much harder than it sounds. And, no matter how many leading questions I ask, sometimes the student just won't understand what I'm trying to lead them to.

I will honestly admit that, after these sessions, I still do not feel confident to tutor on my own. I think that observing some sessions and working on my listening skills will help a bit. Other than that, I will just have to jump in the ring, and try tutoring a student. Hopefully, they won't get a bad grade and then start stalking me or sending death threats!!

–Angela

It's not unusual to feel daunted about starting on your own. But keep in mind that if you had to be thrown into a tutoring situation today and if you didn't have all your skills in place, you'd still do the writer a lot of good, even if all you did was listen to the paper and ask how the writer planned to revise.

I think being in the roles of the tutee and the observer was also extremely helpful.... Being the tutee helped me to understand the struggles the tutee faces and how easy it would be to try to make the tutor take over the paper. You want the tutor to tell you what to do and knowing that is how a tutee often feels will help me as a tutor when in the tutoring session. I will be able to relate to that student. Being the observer was helpful because it really made you aware of the struggles faced in the tutoring session by both the tutee and tutor and helped to shape my methods and my thoughts on how I would handle things in certain situations. The mock tutorials were a great start and definitely helped my confidence in my tutoring abilities. I am excited to start observing and to continue learning from the readings. I think I can do this with a little more preparation. That is the most confidence I have felt yet!

–Kristina

I think that the best way to learn something is to plunge right into the deep end of it. You can get a feel for the water and see how things work by trying different methods. Then you can swim over to the shallow end and survey the experience and say "hey, I was already out there, and even if it looks scary from here, I know that I can do it again." And you can always swim back to the shallow end for reflection. The mock tutorial was sort of a "practice plunge" for me.

–Adele

You'll know as you try these mock tutorials that they're not like the real thing, exactly, because the person you tutor will be anxious to make the tutorial work. But even though there is an air of artificiality, the act of formulating good questions and the satisfaction the writer feels at the end are genuine. Enjoy this process. Your fun is just beginning.

7

TAKING NOTES

Listening to writers read papers can be a challenge if you're not used to it. If you've been observing and if you've been taking part in mock tutorials, then you've had some exercise in listening and careful note-taking as writers read. If in your center you read papers to the writers, then you know what a challenge it can be trying to manage that task and formulate good questions at the same time.

In the past, our trainees have asked us to let them practice by listening to student papers, taking notes, and formulating some questions. We've made that a regular part of our training now, and we'd like to offer you some models—some papers to read and some samples of our trainees' notes and questions.

First, when listening to writers read their papers aloud, or if you are reading them aloud to the writers, it's vital to listen to the whole paper and not jump into a section before you hear the entire thing. A few years ago, we had a bad experience with a writer, an experience that only came out in our staff meeting when we began discussing it. The writer had a problem in her first few paragraphs, and two different tutors worked with her and stopped her, working on the introduction. When a third tutor listened to the entire paper, she found that the paper's main problem lay in the middle, and that the paper didn't really fit the assignment. The first two tutors had become hung up on the first problem and hadn't seen the forest for the trees. Once the writer revised, then, all the problems of the introduction cleared up. So it's important to form an impression of the whole paper.

Taking good notes that you will be able to make sense of later is very important to having a good session. All our tutors have their own unique styles of note-taking. The important thing is to be able to refer to specific sections of the paper that need attention and to include your own reactions. Some tutors like to work on a large sheet of newsprint paper that the writer can write on, too. Some simply write their questions down and have a great capacity for holding the paper and its parts in memory. But most people can't remember an entire paper that well. So here is a model for note-taking that works for lots of tutors. At the top of the page, write down the concerns the writer has expressed, the assignment, and the main idea as the writer has expressed it to you. You'll come back to this when you start asking questions.

Draw a line down the page, about two inches from the left margin.

On the left side, take your own notes: check with a + the things you like. Write down a word or phrase from a sentence you want to return to. Mark with a ? those things you don't quite understand.	At the right of the line, take notes as if you were attending a lecture. These notes will furnish you with a rough outline afterwards, and this outline will allow you to talk about the organization and structure of the paper. Draw lines when you think you hear a paragraph break. You can check with the writer to see if your sense of the organization of the paper matches hers. Get as many details as you can—the more the better.

It's important to explain to the writer what you're doing when you take notes. You don't want the writer to think that you're writing down criticisms, or she will interpret all your writing as trouble for her. Instead, explain that you are going to take notes on her paper as if you were in class, and that when you finish, you should have a rough outline of her paper. This makes it clear to her that she is the expert and that you are learning from her writing. Often writers will ask if they can have your notes, and we always willingly hand them over. Writers seem to appreciate your outline and the comments you might make in the left margin. It takes awhile to get the hang of taking complete notes and getting down all the parts of a paper, so don't expect to be perfect at it right away.

We'll show you some of our trainees' first attempts at note-taking from a paper read aloud to them in class. The following paper was written for a first semester first-year composition course. The paper topic was to do a family history, interviewing family members and relating to a general audience the way in which the family experienced a historical event or period, American or otherwise. Have someone read the following paper to you, so you can practice taking some notes yourself:

The Tale of an Immigrant Farmer

Faith played a larger role in past generations than it does in the present one. In looking over my family history, I found my great-great-great-great grandfather, five generations before me, was a man of strong faith, almost too strong for his own good. His name was Emile Dubois, and the story of his life follows, as well as my reasons for the above claim.

In the mid-nineteenth century, some parts of Europe were quite hellish. Unemployment was a major problem, simply because there were too many people trying to live in the same place at the same time. Due to the population explosion, and a drastic change in the way life from a rural society to a more urban society, land became scarce. Since only one family could be supported by one plot of land, which is relatively small by today's standards, only one child would inherit the entire farm. The other children would have to either marry into a farm, become a migrant worker, or emigrate to the Americas and start from nothing. A young Frenchman by the name of Emile Dubois chose to follow the third option. His father owned a large, four-hundred-year-old farm of thirty-five acres, in Beullot, France; however, the farm could only support his elder sister and her family, so Emile went to join his brother in Illinois. He left in 1846 by way of Le Harve, a major port in Southwestern France, and was fortunate enough to leave before massive emigration took place from that port.

Emile beat the rush and made it to New York with no problem. From New York, Emile joined his younger brother, Modeste, in Lee Center, Illinois, where they both worked in a stone quarry. Between their savings after one year and a loan, the two brothers had enough to buy an eighty-acre farm, at $1.25 an acre, in Bradford, Illinois. The farm was very successful, for after one year, the profits were enough to pay off the mortgage and pay for improvements. One year later, Modeste sold Emile his share of the farm, which by that time had grown into a massive three hundred twenty acres. Illinois has an ideal climate and excellent soil for growing crops, so successful farmers were plentiful, as Modeste displayed when he went on to start his new farm. By the time of his death, Modeste owned fourteen hundred acres of farmland, as well as being the father of fourteen children.

Emile's life after the two brothers split up was a little rougher. He married a young French girl by the name of Sophie Godard, and together they soon had a son, Henry. However, the girl did not like all the hardships the prairie life had to offer, so a little over one year after their marriage, Sophie took Henry and went to live in Chicago. Emile needed a wife and family in order to survive farm life, as my father, Floyd T. Roberts, states in a college essay. He writes, "...the family was the operating economic unit.... The father was the head of the household and its enterprises. He controlled the family's fields...The mother's domain was the house, the livestock, and the children. The children in turn contributed to the economic well-being of the family as soon as they were able" (Roberts, 1). So, being left by his wife left Emile in a sticky moral situation. If he did not remarry, he would soon be forced off his farm. However, his strong Roman Catholic faith would not allow him to remarry. Emile made what I am sure was a painful decision, the decision to remarry. He married a local girl, Roberta Danton, and together they had four boys. Unfortunately, Roberta died after the birth of the fourth, which put Emile back in the same situation as he was before. This time, because he had four boys, he had no choice but to remarry. He married Mrs. Harris, a widow with six children, and together they had four more children, the eldest of which is

Continued

Continued

Clementine Maude Dubois, my great-great-great grandmother.

Mrs. Harris died when Maude was twelve, and Emile Dubois never re-married. I cannot say that I blame him: he must have been shell shocked by that time. Clementine Maude, Emile's daughter mentioned above, describes the hardships in an interview with my father before her death in 1972, "Especially after Ma died, Pa was a moody man…he would eat supper and then sit staring at the fire for the longest time, not talking to anybody…[he was] kind of sad and worn-out like," (Roberts, 5). I would like very much to have talked to him during that stage in his life. What was he thinking? Was he depressed only about his last wife, or about all of them? Perhaps he was in remorse for ever remarrying, and the deaths of his loved ones was part of his punishment from God. If he was so apprehensive of being damned by God about marrying twice, I can imagine that he thought that there was no hope for himself for marrying three times.

Why do past generations seem more devotedly faithful than the present ones? Perhaps it was the hardships they felt and experienced that brought them closer to their faith. Maude stated in the interview with my father, "But it was terrible hard work; sometimes even the women and girls had to work in the fields at harvest time, and keep up with their own chores, too! I wouldn't ever want any of you to have to work as hard as we did then" (Roberts, 6). Why would any man give up a successful future because his faith does not allow it? It would be an interesting perspective, but I can only guess how Emile felt during the remainder of his life.

It is safe to say that past generations were more devotedly faithful than today's society. In a society where a second marriage is as common as a second car, you would have a hard time finding a person in the same situation as Emile. However, due to the drastic change in society and way of life in the past few decades, you cannot go wrong if you are just as moral a person as you can possibly be.

Here were some pages of notes the trainees took.
  Sheri's notes:

Assignment: Engl 001—family history interview—communicate how the period was, based on family experiences.

Comments	Text—paraphrasing, etc.
	GGG Grandfather has too much faith for his own good (at times)
+ Good economic explanation	*Emile Dubois—Loans, hard work, farms, etc.*
+ Why farming was a booming industry	*Illinois soil*
− When were they able?	*The children contributed as soon as they were able*
+ Moving quote and insight	*Daughter of Emile: "I wonder what he was feeling.*

Focus ——————▶	*Why faithfulness and devotion to spouse was important*

Questions: Why did you bring this up at the end of your paper?
Is this essay about hard work/faith in God/or relationships in the past and present?
This painted a very vivid picture, but I'd like to see more development of one main theme.

Notice that Sheri wrote down the assignment (a very important thing to take down). If this had been a real session, she'd have written down the comments the writer made at the start of the session, and his concerns. She then took the notes from the paper on the right side of the sheet and used the signs +, -, and? to indicate things she liked, things she didn't like, and questions she had. She would probably have started the session by telling the writer about the things she liked. She might have held off on the section of the paper she didn't like until she saw how the session went. She felt that the paper wandered from topic to topic, so she wrote some questions that she hoped would lead the writer in that direction.

Here are Kristina's notes:

Interview someone from family—interesting about history of family related to history.
Exhibit historical period w/family member.

Tale of an Immigrant Farmer	*Really like the introduction, of talking about*
Grandfather—5 generations before	*faith. Good idea.*
Mid-19th century ——▶ *conditions*	
Rural ——▶ *urban, land scarce*	*Where?*
Talking about urban life	
Young Frenchmen ——▶ *in France*	
Went to Illinois to join brother	*Modeste: Emile*
Worked in stone quarry	
Bought Farm ——▶ *grew*	
Modeste ——▶ *life after farm split up was*	*Do not even touch on faith until here.*
good	
Emile ——▶ *Bad* ——▶ *need family*	*Too much listing. Confusion here.*
"sticky moral situation"	
Catholic faith	
Decided to marry	
2nd wife died	*Not clear in this area*
Remarried again had 4 boys	
3rd wife died—did not marry again	*Concentrate on marriages* ——▶ *not*
Past generations more faithful	*clear about faith: moral situation*
	◀—— *Need to focus more on this in the*
Today lots of people have multiple marriages	*body; confusing.*

Questions: What do you want to focus on in the paper? Do you feel you have achieved that focus?
What do you mean by faith?
Why was it a "sticky moral situation"? That was not clear to me.
Look at your conclusion. Do you focus on those things in the body of your paper?

Like Sheri, Kristina wrote down the assignment and added the title. Then she took notes down the left side of the page and wrote her questions and comments in the right margin. She wrote her questions at the end. Like Sheri, she felt that the paper needed more focus, and she urged the writer to define the terms "faith" and "sticky moral situation." Like Sheri, she noticed that the conclusion did not seem to fit well with the body of the paper.

Here are Aesha's questions:

- What is your thesis?
- How do you show that Emile's life is an example of this thesis?
- What is the significance of mentioning Emile's brother? How does he fit in with the thesis?
- What do you think is the moral situation of today?
- How is Emile's time different from today?
- What is faith to you? Religious, faith in self, faith in family?
- How does Emile overcome his "Sticky moral situation" and still hold on to his faith?

Any of these questions would be an excellent way of starting this session and getting the writer thinking about good ways to revise his paper.

Here is another paper—same paper topic, same class. Trainees' notes and questions follow.

Newlyweds at War

The year was 1966. My parents, Donna and Mark Molloy, had just been wed. Mark was in his last year of law school at the University of Minnesota and Donna, at the ripe age of nineteen, was working part time as a lab technician. The newlyweds looked eagerly at their futures together. They planned to travel the world, take time to be together and simply enjoy one another's company. Little did they know, that the Vietnam conflict would disrupt their new found happiness and turn their world upside down.

The R.O.T.C. program put Mark through college. After law school, he was required to fill a two year commitment to the army. His friends from college, on the same program, fulfilled their duties immediately following college. They were assigned to countries like Europe, performing tasks such as couriers. Mark assumed that when his time came to serve he would be doing likewise.

Mark graduated from law school in June of 1967 and proceeded to take the Bar Exam on July 15, 1967. Mark then received notice that he was commissioned to Fort Benning, Georgia on July 28, 1967 to act as a First Lieutenant. The position entailed being an infantry officer with army intelligence and going through eight rigorous weeks of infantry school. The couple uprooted from their St. Paul apartment and landed in a short-time lease, cockroach infested housing project in the humidity of the south. My father was up before the sun, spent hours on end in the fields and rarely returned home before dark. For young Donna, this meant days filled with boredom and loneliness. She met up with other wives in the same position. In their new community, they taught each other craft projects and had solitaire marathons to fill the time.

The eight weeks was nearly over and Donna was thrilled that they would be moving on. Although Vietnam was a realistic threat for my parents, they assumed that my father would only go as far as Washington to serve as an advisor. They did not imagine that he would actually be sent to Vietnam to fight. The mail on September 6 brought a pleasant surprise, Mark had passed the Bar Exam. A prosperous future was in sight. Unfortunately, the very next day's mail was not so kind. Surprisingly, Mark was ordered to Vietnam and Donna was faced with the fact that she would be left alone, thousands of miles from her husband for only one year.

To prepare for the voyage, the couple moved to Baltimore, Maryland. There, at Fort Holbird, Mark and Donna teamed with other lawyers and their wives who were going through the same horrible, but very realistic situation. As the men attended Army Intelligence courses, the women began to form bonds. Luckily, these friendships provided Donna with the strength and support she needed to see her husband off to war.

Time passed quickly and before the couple knew it, they were forced to face December 8, 1967. Mark and Donna exchanged their good byes with thoughts of the future haunting their minds. Mark boarded a plane for Saigon and Donna waved good bye with tears welting in her eyes. She stared at his face with a deep fondness, wondering, if God-forbid, she would ever see it again.

In the days that followed, Donna moved back to Minnesota and continued work as a lab technician. She shared an apartment with her cousin, and three friends. The doctor that Donna was working for decided to practice elsewhere, not only did she not have her husband, now she did not have a job. My dad's father felt compassion for his newest daughter and convinced her to move in with their family (the youngest three of seven children were still living at home). They shared the same loneliness as Donna, and together, they worked through Mark's absence.

Mark was living among the Vietnamese, Mekong Delta, serving as an advisor with seven other Americans. He was in charge of intelligence missions. When weapons were confiscated from the enemy, my father was in charge of inspecting them and determining their type. He also flew in helicopters, taking pictures of incoming B-52's.

The mail became vital in keeping communication alive between Mark and the family at home. The news broadcasts would run and the family kept their fingers crossed, waiting for Mark's letters, often delayed by the mail service. My grandfather would send tapes of himself and the family, along with anyone of town members, to Mark. If the weather agreed, Mark would sit on the roof and listen to the familiar voices, over and over and

Continued

Continued

over. In turn, Mark would send slides of Vietnam with a tape to accompany it. In one slide, Mark took a picture of the gate outside his home that had been hit. My grandfather recognized the gate from previous slides and it was times like these that sent the entire family into panic.

In August of 1968, after being separated for eight months, Mark and Donna were given the opportunity to see each other. Mark had been granted a one week "R&R" (rest and relaxation) period. They met in Hawaii with a couple they had met at Fort Holibird. They had seven short days to catch up on all of the events that had passed since Mark's departure. The last day of their vacation came upon them and once again, Donna had to repeat the dreaded good bye at the airport. This time, however, she had hope that she would be seeing him again soon.

Once Mark was back in Vietnam, he had to deal with dysentery. He got the disease from eating the food, cooked by the Vietnamese. Although the bout with sickness put a scare on Mark and the family, they knew the end of Mark's army commitment was in sight. On December 8, 1968, Mark flew home, leaving his memories of war behind. Unfortunately, it was a leap year and it took one day longer for him to return. My grandmother always said that God must have been on their side because not only was December 8 the day her son returned, it was a holy day as well.

One last step had to be taken before the couple could return to normalcy. They were back together, and that was worth anything the last months of my father's commitment required. Once again, it was necessary that they move. This time Mark and Donna wound up at Fort Lenardward in Missouri, were Mark served as an intelligence officer. He was now a captain and his final duty was to provide security clearance for new recruits.

July of 1969 came along and they were free! Mark and Donna moved to St. Cloud, MN. In September of 1969, Mark was granted a partnership with a local firm. At last, their futures were falling into place. In the fall of 66, they had no idea what was ahead. Their marriage had survived the strain of a war, and they knew now that they had the strength to tackle anything their futures may hold.

Jessi's notes:

Paper topic ⟶ *History paper—historical concept through use of family narrative.*

"Newlyweds at War"

-parents just married in '66—dad was w/ROTC and Nam interrupts marriage.

Sent to Georgia to be lieutenant 8 wks

Passes bar, then ordered to Nam

moved to Baltimore

went to war

Dec 8, 1967 he leaves

Mail as vital communication, tapes of family members—slides sent back home from Nam

In 1968—they met for 1 week of R&R

Dec. he returns home. They move to Missouri

1969 moved to Minnesota—things were back to normal

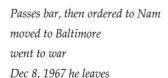

They can now handle anything.

Notice that Jessi marks the divisions of the paper (as she hears them) with arrows. Later she can use these arrows to ask the writer if these indicate the true paragraph breaks.

A number of trainees wondered what the focus of the paper was and felt ill at ease that the writer depicted the story as such a happy-ever-after sort of tale. Kristina asked some hard questions that might have made the writer deepen her inquiry into her parents' history:

- Did your father suffer from any postwar stress that made returning to the States challenging in some way?
- How did your father feel for the year he was in Vietnam?
- Has he ever given you a vivid description of what things were like in Vietnam?

As the class discussed this paper, we found that we all wondered why this writer chose to depict the war as a scary inconvenience, and we felt that the paper might have benefited from some more details about what else might have been going on during this time: How many from their town died in the war? What were the casualty rates? How lucky was her father, actually? They speculated that the story she told is the story she *was* told, and that perhaps all the members of his family might have agreed that this was the story they could live with. They discussed being sensitive to the writer's sensitivities and having respect for family privacy.

Our notes are often our prompts for what kinds of questions to ask. Remember to come back to any concerns the writer had and address them first, either by dealing with them or by assuring the writer that you'll come back to them. When you look at your notes, remember to put higher-order concerns first. Sometimes the first thing you notice on your page of notes is something about a word or expression that sounds wrong to you. Remember to deal with the topic, its suitability to the assignment, the support, and the organization first. Then come back to that word, if it seems appropriate. As you become an experienced tutor, you'll feel good about your ability to take notes on a session, whatever system you develop for it.

Here are some additional papers you can practice with:

Lerner/LIB111

Group Written Summary Assignment Sheet

Instructions: For the Group Written Summary Assignment, your group will write a 250- to 400-word summary of either "On Racist Speech" by Charles Lawrence (Barnet and Badeau, pp. 26–30) or "Protecting Freedom of Expression on Campus" by Derek Bok (Barnet and Badeau, pp. 31–33). Your summary should possess the important characteristics of brevity, objectivity, completeness, and accuracy and should include:

- a version of the author's thesis
- the main points of the essay
- selected important examples or details

Intended audience: Imagine that your reader has not read the essay you are summarizing.

First draft to be completed in class—Tuesday, Sept. 29.

Final draft due—Tuesday, Oct. 6. After getting feedback in class on Sept. 29, your group will have a chance to revise your draft before final submission. Feedback will also include your entire group signing up for and attending a writing center session (WB 12 C&D, 732-2091).

Evaluation Criteria: Your final draft should be typed, double-spaced, with one-inch margins. Evaluation will be based upon how well your draft meets the criteria of effective summaries (brevity, objectivity, completeness, and accuracy), as well as general essay criteria including logical organization, appropriate style, and correct mechanics.

10/7/98

Group Essay 1

Where do We Draw the Line?

In this essay "Protecting Freedom of Expression on the Campus" Derek Bok focuses on the controversy of whether hanging Confederate flags at a private institution is legal under the First Amendment. The incident which prompted this issue occured at Harvard University where two students chose to display Confederate flags in public. This problem was then further escalated when another student displayed a swastika.

In the next three paragraphs Bok takes a stand against these symbols. He declares that although under law the flags are protected they provoke feelings of discomfort and pain while only satisfying a few. He calls these actions as "insensitive and unwise" and for the part unwarrented.

In the sixth paragraph Bok wrestles with the fact that although our community may dislike certain jestures or symbols, such as the flags, we are bound by the constitution in making our final decision.

Bok then proves that the Confederate flag and the swastika are protected under the First Amendment, and can-not be deemed unlawful simply because the feelings of other members of the community may be offended. He does so by making reference to the Supreme Court rulings.

In the next two paragraphs Bok provides evidence backing the First Amendment. Two reasons why Bok believes that censorship is unwarrented constitutes primarily on deciding upon the degree of which a particular action is considered offensive. Then, when trying to determine what to censor, Bok reasons that to much time would be taken and excitement aroused in making and testing the limits of these decisions.

In the concluding paragraphs the author proceeds to lay out solutions which could effectively be used in the Harvard case. Some solutions that Bok provide include ignoring the situation (hence lessening the amount of controversy on campus), involving administration and faculty, and educating students. By following these guidelines, Bok concludes, that our communities will become "truly understanding and supportive."

Group "Money"

10/08/98

"Expression of Rights on Campus"

In Derek Bok's essay "Protecting Freedom of Expression on the Campus" he discusses the ideas of freedom of speech and the rights of a student on the college campus. Written while he was president of Harvard, it was first

Continued

Continued

published in the Boston Globe in 1991. It was in response to a situation in which two Harvard students hung a Confederate flag in public view. Another student, in retaliation of the flag, displayed a swastika. Bok's opinion on whether or not to prohibit such actions is that it is not exactly the best way to handle such situations. He feels that censorship is very dangerous because it ceases communication and that it may be better to ignore the situation rather than act against it.

Trying to avoid racial tension has been a factor in college for years. The first amendment makes keeping control of racial tension difficult because it protects the students by giving them the right to free speech. Bok thought that this certain situation was very wrong, but that it wasn't correct to just prohibit doing it. Not only does this go against the students right to free speech, but it also doesn't allow the students to discuss and possibly solve the issue on their own.

Events, like the one at Harvard, have raised many concerns due to the nature of the negative connotations that objects like the flags represent. Many students felt that Harvard should force the removal of such racial symbols. Others felt that these symbols are simply an example of freedom of speech, which in this case, should be protected and allowed. Bok believes that the university could at-tempt to resolve the situation by creating regulations that would punish offenders, in order to protect students from such racial speech. He also thinks that there also might be alternative routes in solving the problem.

According to Bok, the students of Harvard knew that hanging such symbols of this nature would cause some commotion, and harass and intimidate their fellow students. Even though these expressions were wrong morally they are protected under the first amendment. This raises the argument of whether to enforce the right of free speech or to keep peace among community. According to the Supreme Court's rulings, the right of free speech shall be enforced whether or not it offends people. It also states that this is enforced in all agencies such as colleges and universities.

Bok suggests that the best solution might be education and persuasion of more moral behavior from the students. He thinks that this may work better than prohibiting the negative acts. Bok's final thoughts are, when dealing with a situation that involves the harassing of others but is protected under the first amendment we should keep communication open. Officials and students should take the proper actions to educate rather than ridicule, through these acts an understanding should be created and such violations would cease.

LIB111/Lerner—Fall 1998

Essay #2 Assignment Sheet

For Essay #2, you will be writing a summary and critique of one of the readings from *Critical Thinking, Reading, & Writing.* You can choose any of the essays at the end of Chapters 3 or 4. (Note: Refer to sample student critique in Chapter 4 for a model of this type of essay.)

Your Purpose: To present an author's position on his or her topic and either support or refute that point of view.

Intended Audience: Assume that your reader is *not* familiar with the reading you have chosen.

Structure: A summary/critique contains the follows components:

Introduction: You will introduce the reading and its author, "state the reading's main argument and the point(s) you intend to make about it," and give your reader any background material that is essential to understand the context of the reading and your critique.

Summary: As you did in your group essay, you need to summarize the reading, attaining brevity, clarity, completeness, and accuracy.

Analysis of and response to the argument: As Barnet and Bedau point out in Chapter 4 (pp. 73–76), your analysis should consider the author's thesis, purpose, methods, and persona. You can use your analysis to point out the flaws or strengths of the author's argument. Your critique should also be clear as to whether you agree or disagree with the author's views, and you need to support your opinion with persuasive examples from what you have read or experienced.

Conclusion: Reiterate for your audience *your* reason for writing and your evaluation of the reading you have chosen.

Length of final draft: 3 to 4 pages, double-spaced typed, w/one-inch margins.

Evaluation Criteria: (1) Accuracy, brevity, conciseness, and objectivity of your summary; (2) detailed evidence to support your larger points; (3) a logical structure overall, including an introduction that "sets the scene" for your reader, establishes your topic generally, and indicates or forecasts what your essay will be about and how you will approach that topic; (4) effective paragraph placement and development—each paragraph builds upon what came before and leads naturally with transition words and phrases to what will follow; (5) a minimum of errors in grammar, usage, spelling, and punctuation.

Rough draft due—Thursday, Oct. 15. Your rough draft need not be typed. Note that I will not grade your rough draft but instead give you feedback in order for you to strengthen your final draft. If you prefer that I tape-record my comments, please submit an audiotape with your rough draft. Your groups will also provide feedback to your rough drafts.

Final draft due—Tuesday, Oct. 27.

Also, while I'm requiring that each of you go to the writing center once during the semester, all can benefit from getting writing center feedback at any stage of your writing process. Call 732-2092 or go to WB-12, White Building basement, to make an appointment.

Katie Delongchamp

November 3, 1998

Essay #2

Looking for a Wife

Judy Brady wrote an essay entitled "I Want a Wife" which gives the point of view that women have a very difficult way of living. Although it seems awkward at first, Brady is commenting on the hardship that a woman encounters once she is married.

Brady informs the audiece that is married and has children. She then tells about a friend of hers who had just recently been divorced. He wants a new wife. Brady says she wants a wife as well, and gives the reader the reasons behind this. By giving the example of how this man wants a "new" wife, Brady is setting the tone of the essay, which is that women have a huge responsibility once they are married, and that men should be lucky that women work so hard in marriages. Brady then gives the reasons why men should feel so lucky that they have wives.

Some of the jobs that Brady's wife would have includes keeping track of the children, which includes making their appointments, making sure they eat healthy and keep clean, have clean clothes, and have fun. Her wife would also take care of the children when they are sick, arrange for the children when they need something important. This wife must also be willing to miss time at work if need be. There are also the chores around the house that Brady's wife would have to be responsible for.

Cooking, cleaning the house, ironing the clothes, and taking care of the sick are also duties that Brady's wife must be able to have. And Brady's wife also must not complain about the incredible responsibility placed on her. By pointing out all the things that Brady wants her wife to do, she is showing the audience how much an actual wife must do, and how much of a responsibility being a wife is. All the things Brady wants her wife to do are in fact things that she does. And by the tone of these paragraphs, Brady is resentful of her husband and of her life. She goes on further about what her wife would be like, which is in fact what she is expected to do.

Another feature Brady's wife would have would be sensitivity. They would be understanding when it came to sexual conflicts, and would take complete responsibility for all methods of birth control. She also wants a wife who will not cheat on her, and will be faithful. Finally, Brady wants to be able to replace her wife if she wants, and start fresh, just like her friend who got divorced. All of these things Brady wants in a wife are actually what every guy wants.

By pointing out all the things she wants in her "wife", Brady is actually showing the reader what men expect women to do. And while women are expected to do all these things, men seem to have no responsibility, in her opinion. This can be summed up when Brady talks about how if she wants she should be able to have a new wife. And I feel that this point of view is immoral.

There are many men in the world that just leave their families behind because they see somebody else they want. They do not care about what they have, and instead start anew. But what these people should realize is just how lucky they are to have such wonderful women in their lives. When guys leave their families for this reason, I get a sick feeling in my stomach. This, to me, is one of the most awful and unexplainable thins a person can do. Leaving you own children and wife behind is reprehensible, and sickening, and just plain wrong.

Brady sums up her essay by asking the reader why they would not want a wife. Wives do everything men ask them to, according to Brady. They do all the jobs mentioned before, and more. They are socially, physically, and emotionally responsible. This essay is Brady venting frustration stemming from the fact that women are expected to have so many responsibilities, and men are expected to have basically none. She also says that she has no time for herself. If she did have this wife, it would basically be a nanny. And I agree. Being a woman is extremely difficult, and Brady sums this up logically and concisely.

This essay was an eye-opener to me, and would be to any other women who read it. If many young women would read this essay, I sincerely believe that they would have second thoughts about marriage and making the commitment. Brady's view is very similar to many other women's opinion's I know, such as my aunt's or even my own mother's. Although I have not sincerely thought about marriage, due to the fact that I am only 18 years old, I may consider delaying the process. Hopefully, the way of life that Brady gives the audience will not be the way I live. And if it is, then I do not want to be a wife!

Anne Reynolds

Lib 111A

November 3, 1998

Not Emotional Enough

Vita Wallace, author of "Give Children the Vote," looks for support in her fight to include children in the election process. However, despite her attempts, I feel her arguments are weak and unpersuasive. Wallace presents four major points in her essay. She feels that denying children the right to vote prevents them from defending their "rights as citizens to life, liberty, and the pursuit of happiness." She also argues that the essence of democracy is letting people vote for whichever they choose, even if it happens to be the "wrong" candidate. Next, Wallace defends children's irresponsibility by reasoning that children are not allowed to solve their problems responsibly—such as through the courts or legislature. Finally, she assures that "the vast majority of children would not attempt to vote before they are ready."

Continued

Continued

The essay begins as the author sets the stage by telling her personal experience on the matter. She explains that she first became interested in the topic of children's rights when she heard of laws being passed to prohibit high school dropouts from getting drivers' licenses. The reason this caught her attention is that Vita Wallace is a home schooler, which means she has never been to school. Due to the fact that she has had success without ever attending school, she feels other children should not be penalized if they choose not to attend school. Extensive constitutional and historical research has convinced her that children will continue to be treated unfairly and punished for practicing the few legal rights they have, such as dropping out of school, if they are not given the right to elect their representatives as adults are. Her research has also led her to believe the following points. In the United States it is overlooked that children are the most regulated people. School attendance laws, child labor laws, and alcohol and cigarette laws—in addition to all of the laws that affect adults—bind children. She points out that the abolition of slavery did not end the exploitation of black people. As a race, they needed to be allowed to vote and to have the ability to bring lawsuits against their employers, just as children do. Wallace feels that laws forcing children to attend school and prohibiting them from working are necessary to prevent exploitation. However, she also feels that these laws take away children's "rights as citizens to life, liberty, and the pursuit of happiness."

Because those under eighteen do not have the right to vote, young people are being denied the most effective tool available to initiate a change in democracy. Wallace's suggestion is that citizens under eighteen are not denied or abridged the right to vote on account of age. It has been brought up that letting loose on society a large group of new voters would be dangerous because the new voters might not vote sensibly. Wallace does not believe a large group of new voters would be dangerous to society. She reminds the reader that the whole idea behind democracy is letting people vote for whomever they want. Democratic society is supposed to have risks. Large segments of the population who are not allowed or are not likely to vote are often treated badly, so the more people who vote the better.

Wallace also claims the reason behind children's irresponsibility is that they are not allowed to solve their problems responsibly, such as through the courts or legislature. Yet she feels children would be responsible in the process of voting. What she suggests is that children should be allowed to grow into their vote at a rate that suits them individually. They should neither be forced to vote nor hindered from the voting process. Wallace feels the majority of children would not attempt to vote until they were interested. And she says interest falls hand in hand with readiness.

Wallace's essay has an overall emotional appeal for a couple of reasons. First she begins by relating her own personal experience to the matter at hand. Second, in reminding the reader of children's inability to take part in changing the laws, she looks for sympathy from adults to initiate their desire to help fight for children's rights.

Although emotional appeal is a strong tool, I was not persuaded to believe that children should be given the right to vote. Wallace bases her argument—not being allowed to vote prevents children from defending their rights as citizens to life, liberty and the pursuit of happiness—on her personal experience. She explains how the prohibition of drivers' licenses to high school dropouts would indeed interfere with her right to happiness. However, it is a weak argument because she is trying to make a generalization. I think these laws serve as a motivation for kids to remain in school, and for the large majority of children, remaining in school is the best choice they could make. Wallace is correct about the essence of democracy, however she is making an assumption. She assumes that children would take voting seriously. I can hardly imagine that children's minds are capable of comprehending the responsibilities that coincide with governing a nation. Sure, children would vote if they were allowed to, but very few if any would understand the meaning behind what they were voting for. It is far more likely that children would vote because mommy and daddy do it and they think it is fun. Just because children are not allowed to solve their problems through the court systems or the legislature does not mean they would all of a sudden be considered responsible if they were allowed to use the system. There are many other ways to resolve problems responsibly if they were allowed to use the system. There are many other ways to resolve problems responsibly that children do not take advantage of, and being allowed to vote would not change this. Finally, Wallace argues that children would not vote until they were interested and therefore ready. However, I disagree with this also. For example, consider the idea of allowance. When children are given money, we will assume it is because they are interested and have asked their parents for an allowance, but does it mean they are ready to spend it responsibly? Definitely not, most children are known to spend their allowance on candy and toys. Voting is a serious task that requires responsibility no matter how you look at it. And childhood is meant to be a carefree and enjoyable time of life, so I do not feel children should be plagued by the responsibility of voting. Wallace also points out that it is overlooked that children are the most regulated people in the United States. So, if most children do not even realize they are so regulated, and probably they will not realize it until they are near voting age anyway, there is no point in changing the age limit.

Joel Sanford

11/3/98

Up In Arms

In "Just Take Their Guns Away," James Wilson, professor of management and public policy at UCLA, explains why tougher gun control laws

Continued

Continued

will not work to slow down the illegal use of firearms in crime. He also gives some valid ways to decrease the illegal use of firearms. I think that Wilson is correct in his judgment that new and stricter laws will not work in the right way. If somebody really wants a gun, it can be easily obtained illegally through devious means.

Wilson feels that more legal restraints on the legal purchase of guns won't mean less illegal use of the weapons. The reduction of these purchases will also decrease the ability of citizens to defend themselves. Wilson thinks that the main purpose of new gun laws should be to minimize the number of people who unlawfully carry guns. To do this, he feels that by increasing the number of street frisks that are performed by the police force would help to confiscate illegal weapons.

Street frisks are risky. There is a fine line between what is a legal "search and seizure" and what is not. It has been shown that the Supreme Court allows search and seizure if there is "reasonable suspicion," or the person is on parole or probation. Therefore, the police must be helped out by being given a list of people on parole or probation in their area and they must be trained to recognize actions that constitute "reasonable suspicion."

Self-defense is a very good form of deterrence. Wilson says that the National Crime Survey reported that people defending themselves with a weapon were less likely to lose property in a robbery, or to be injured in an assault. Burglars are aware that people in America are more likely to have weapons in the house. This is why they are more likely to rob an occu-pied house in Europe than in America because residents there rarely have firearms.

Control advocates say that defense equals injury. Wilson counters this point by saying that the rate of fatal gun accidents has actually been going down, whereas the number of gun ownerships has been increasing. He also points out that the NRA (National Rifle Association) makes a mistake when it tries to get stricter punishments for those who use weapons in crimes. He thinks that these add-ons will be used for prosecutors to bargain with, if not, the judge will rarely use them because they are so severe.

Criminals end up carrying guns anyway. They carry them to protect themselves from other criminals. This just escalates until everyone is carrying a gun. The majority of them will most likely be illegal.

New innovations in the science field can be used to help out in the battle. There are metal detectors in airports to deter carrying weapons onto planes. These must be made so that the police can use them on the street to pick up offenders.

I think that Wilson makes many great points in this essay. I believe a lot of what he says and I feel he is right. I think that if there wasn't enough red tape, criminals would easily be able to purchase the guns and then use them in crimes. There needs to be a happy medium somewhere. As Wilson says, the bottom line is that the illegal guns must be removed from the streets so they are not used in crimes. I feel very strongly that Wilson is right that stricter gun laws, which means more red tape, will not help the war on handguns. Guns are a problem in the wrong hands, their power must not be taken lightly.

I think that it starts in childhood. I was taught never to mistreat a firearm, and it sunk in when I was that young.

I know the dangers that are involved with weapons, and I don't think other people do fully understand what they are doing with them. They just end up ruining it for all of us.

LIB111/Lerner

Essay #3 Assignment Sheet

Fall 1998

Essay #3 will require you to synthesize various views on a single topic, presenting those views to a reader, and then arguing for the superiority of one point of view.

Directions:

From the packet of readings I will hand out, choose as your topic either the use of herbal medications or the legalization of marijuana for medicinal purposes. Your task in this essay will be to present to *an uninformed reader* the background on your topic (why the topic is important, what the view of each side is, and what evidence is presented to support those views) and then to argue for one side or another *or* a synthesized position that draws upon the best ideas of both sides (see Carl Rogers's essay "Communication: Its Blocking and Its Facilitation," pp. 326–333 of *Critical Thinking, Reading, & Writing*). You will need to present evidence supporting *your* view, whether that means drawing from your readings, presenting your own experience, or including authoritative sources outside of the material I give you. Remember that your criticism of a particular point of view is strengthened if you take issue with *how* that argument is presented, not merely what it says.

Ultimately, this will be an essay of at least three or four pages that focuses your reader with an effective introduction, accurately and concisely presents the views of each side of the issue, and then presents the view you determine to be superior via evidence and analysis.

We will be developing more specific grading criteria in class.

Note: You will need to cite your sources accurately using correct MLA citation format; you will also need to include a Works Cited page.

Deadlines:

Rough Draft Due November 19—Please bring *three* additional copies for group critique.

Final Draft Due December 1 (tentatively)

Ronald Brankly   Lib 111A

12/4/98

Hell No, Herbs Won't Go

This topic is the selling of herbal drugs. It is an extensive business and an old-time style of apothecary. The debate is on whether phytomedicines should be sold or not. The pro side says yes (although it seems very vague at times) while the opponents say no because phytomedicines are very dangerous to consume.

The voices against the sale of plant drugs were Peter de Smet, a clinical pharmacologist, and Virginia Murray, a toxicologist at the National Medical Toxicology Unit, in Cathy Sears' article, *Selling Drugs* (Sears, Cathy. "Selling Drugs..." *News Scientist.* 4 November 1995). De Smet states that the main problem isn't that fact that the herbs are being sold, rather, it is that the herbs being used as food and vitamin supplements are not tested before being distributed to the open market. This has caused quite a few deaths because the herbs can either interact with prescription drugs or they can block the body's natural system from doing the organ's natural functions. This is because the cost for drug testing of herbal-extract medicines is very expensive and very time-consuming. (Usually, dozens of different tests need to be run on humans with different ailments.) It is also because the government does not have policies that properly protect untested plants and botanicals from unknowing consumers; and this is the result of the inability to patent plants (because anyone can grow any type of plant). Murray also states that the issue of not testing the

chemicals in plants can make a difference. For example, the same kind of plant grown in different areas can have different amounts of chemical strength. This can result in death, as it did for two people in Britain and another thirty in other parts of Europe who took a phytomedicinal product that was unknowingly poisonous. Both answers are clear by having the U.S. government put more restrictions on herbal drugs that are over-the-counter.

The second article for those against plant medicine is Judy Foreman, author of the column Health Sense (Foreman, Judy. "Health Sense." *The Boston Globe.* 26 Oct 1998. C1, C4–5). She starts the essay dramatically with questions that make you think and which are related to the article itself. In addition to attacking the Government, as in the former article, she also mentions some of the different drugs and their side effects (e.g., blood thinners, antidepressants, sedatives, etc.) on different parts of the human body. She then presents the theory of one phytomedicine (St. John's wort) acting equally as efficient as two different types of prescription drugs (MAO inhibitor, which increases production of brain chemicals such as seratonin, and an antidepressant that prevents absorption of seratonin). If this is the case, then adverse side effects of both drugs should be reported. From the second article, *Supplement Standards Are Written,* she writes that Congress passed the Dietary Supplement Health and Education Act. This states that the FDA can take a dietary supplement off the market *only* if it finds conclusive proof that the product does harm in some way.

Andrew Weil, author of *Spontaneous Healing,* a book that explains how to cure common ailments using herbal plants, defends the pro side of this argument. He explains that herbs have the ability to help the human body without the reliance on powerful chemical drugs that can sometimes make the foreign body become stronger with their use. The herbs boosting the immune system have a low strength that can help the body to absorb them with little resistance do them. Weil says that there are a few cases where people have died, but the majority of people have been cured or most of their symptoms have been alleviated. The best way to take medicines of this kind is either by tincture or extract mixed with water and alcohol, or by the freeze-dried method, which will "preserve the odor and color of culinary herbs" (Weil, Andrew. "Herbal Medicine—Reclaiming a Safer Way to Heal." *HealthFacts.* 21 June 1996: p4.). The article also warns the reader/consumer to read the label and check that it says it is standardized. Dr. Varro Tyler at Purdue University says that, without this, the drug could be useless, dangerous, or only helpful when consumed in large quantities, such as with garlic cloves. Another problem with the utilization is that there are no formal courses taught on this subject and no proper book that can be used as a standard. Weil finally concludes that it would save the health care system money by having doctors prescribe more natural drugs and less chemical ones.

I believe that the herbal medicines should be used but Congress should give the FDA more power to research this subject further. If this could be done, many more drugs that are harmful to people could be taken off the market. However I do agree with the points made by the opponents when they stated that some European countries, such as Britain, are stricter with their standards of herbs being sold. According to *Selling Drugs,* "Britain …insists that the herbal medicines match its own standards for conventional over-the-counter products and prescriptions drugs." If we [the U.S.] used this system, there would be no problem with accidental herb poisonings. This FDA should also set up more companies that test these OTCs. Although the FDA has gained a little power with the Dietary Act, it still has a long way to go before it can make any effective change.

In the end, it is the buyer who makes the ultimate choice on the drug's dependence and safety. It is they who will spend their hard-earned money to buy the product, they who will take, and they who will have to live with the consequences. For better or worse.

8

TUTORING FOR REAL

Sometimes our first tutoring sessions come before we really feel ready for them. Sara, a trainee, was in the writing center observing a session. Just as the session was ending, Craig, a first-year student, showed up and just wanted someone to spend five minutes with him as he got ready to write his first lab report. All the experienced tutors were busy. But Sara had just finished observing a session. Craig just wanted to talk to anyone about this assignment, and in fact, he said that if no one was available, he'd just go to his dorm, because lots of sophomores lived there.

It was still fairly early in Sara's training, but she felt all right about just answering five minutes' worth of questions. Craig needed to know about finding and citing on-line sources, and Sara was able to answer his questions well. He said he'd be coming in a lot with his papers, and Sara ended her first session feeling confident.

ANXIETIES

Sometimes trainees feel hesitant to dive in, and if they have a choice, some will put off their first solo sessions. Stewart discusses this anxious feeling in a reflective paper.

When I first started in English 192 [the Marquette training course], I eagerly awaited the delivery of the "formula." I became convinced that there was indeed a formula when I read a letter from an English 192 student from last year, and it advised me not to worry about learning the formula because there is none. (What a way to throw me off!) I expected that sometime around the sixth week of the term, the instructor would come and say, "Okay, now that we've rooted out all the losers, here is the super-secret formula for successfully tutoring anybody in any situation." I imagined that this formula would come in the form of a five-page handout and that these few sheets of paper would hold an algorithm with which I could successfully conduct any tutoring situation from freshman English to doctoral dissertations and that it would require almost no thinking. The semester wore on, and we did read lots of different books and dozens of articles about tutoring, but none came close to unlocking the mysteries of tutoring or the greater mysteries of writing. No formula! (Not even from Jeff Brooks!)

If you've done some mock tutorials and if you've observed some sessions, you probably wonder if you'll ask the right questions or if you're ready, or good enough. You're ready and you're good enough if you respect the writer and if you are willing to let the writer do the work. If you let the writer read the paper to you, and if you start the session by asking the writer, "All right, now that you've read it to me, what do you want to do next?" then you've got the session off to a good start.

Donald Murray, in an article called "The Listening Eye," talks about his good experiences as a writing teacher, asking his students the following questions and then just sitting back, putting his feet on his desk, and waiting for answers.

- What did you learn from this piece of writing?
- What do you intend to do in the next draft?
- What surprised you in the draft?
- Where is the piece of writing taking you?
- What do you like best in the piece of writing?
- What questions do you have of me?

If you think it will give you confidence, feel free to write these questions down and keep them with you, but we believe that you'll know some good questions to ask on your own.

FIRST SOLO FLIGHTS

First tutoring experiences range from wonderful to scary. Here are two accounts of first-time tutoring experiences:

My first session was with an 001 student who was working on the fourth paper assignment, which focused upon the presentation of a persuasive argument. I felt that we established a good rapport right from the beginning. In fact, we caught the same elevator up to the fourth floor of Monitor Hall, and had talked about the fact that this was her first visit to the writing center, that she was a first-year student and volleyball player and so forth; we did not discover that we would be working together until I consulted the appointment book. The fact that we had already engaged in some initial conversation and felt comfortable with each other made the situation ideal for a tutoring session (especially for my first one: I was nervous anyway, and it was nice to be able to work with someone that I knew—however briefly—in some other context).

The student had chosen a topic for her paper (the possible health benefits of marijuana for patients with terminal illnesses), had done a great deal of research, and had done a lot of writing. The problem was that although she had written out her three main arguments, and constructed passages anticipating and refuting possible counterarguments, she didn't know how to organize the paper. Accordingly, she did not have a cohesive rough draft, but instead several pieces of paper detailing her various points, all of which were well-written but not in any way connected to each other.

At first I was a little baffled as to how to proceed. I started out by having her tell me what she thought her thesis statement and her three main points were, and writing them all down. Then I had her read me the different portions of her paper so I could get a better idea of how she had planned to argue her points.

While I was listening to the student read, an enormous sense of responsibility for her and her paper hit me. What if I gave her bad advice? What if my advice resulted in her getting a bad grade? What made me an authority on any of this? Upon reflection, I think the reason for these anxieties lay in the fact that I myself have often had difficulties with organization. When the student told me at the beginning of the session that she had a clear idea of what she wanted to say but was having a hard time finding a logical way of organizing her points, since they all seemed interrelated, I saw myself in her confusion. Initially, then, instead of making me more confident to tutor someone having this problem, the fact that I had experienced a similar difficulty in writing made me think that, because I myself hadn't found a solution, I couldn't begin to advise others on how to do it.

Time ran out on my agonizing, however, when she finished reading the paper and looked expectantly at me. Forced to say something, anything, I looked back down at my notes and asked the first question that came to mind, about whether some information that she had included under one point might really work better to support another. That first question, and her ready, engaged response, was all it took, and soon we both were able to discuss ways in which she could make her three points distinct from each other, but simultaneously in support of one thesis. We also talked about smooth transitions between her arguments, and tried to think of ways in which one of the arguments could be seen as providing a different angle on another, which would allow her to move from one focus to the other with ease.

When the session ended, the student told me, "This was fun," and said that what had helped more than anything was just being able to talk about her ideas, and thereby see the connections between them, as well as possible ways of organizing them. I, too, left the session feeling I had gained something: a positive first tutoring experience, and insight into my own processes as a writer. By seeing another person's struggles with organization, and helping her to work through them, I was able to recognize the same problem in myself and (hopefully) bolster my own confidence for dealing with the problem—a gain which would be tested by my next essay assignment.

–Caroline Goyette

Caroline could relate well to the writer she worked with, and her session went very well. Sometimes it can be reassuring to the writers if we tell them that we struggle with the same things they do—anything from procrastination to dangling modifiers—and that, like them, we are working on our own writing. You'll know from the context of the session whether this is the right thing to do or not.

Not all first sessions go as well or give such good insights, and we have to go easy on ourselves if our first session isn't all we hope it will be. This reflective essay tells the story of Stephanie's first independent session:

Last night was one of those impending deadline panic nights. Tonight is another. It's one of those weeks when there is a test on Tuesday and a paper due every other day of the week (and that's not including this one)…In some ways, nights like tonight comfort me in my struggle to understand the tutoring process. After all, I *am* those students I will be tutoring. I'm panicked, full of coffee, and searching for clarity. I'm trying to take notice of and discover my "felt sense."[1] In other ways, nights like these instill a sense of anxiety about tutoring because I am truly the students' peer. How can I help another when I have trouble with my own papers—when I can't decide if a semicolon goes here or there?

I think these feelings of confidence and anxiety manifested themselves in my first tutoring session. When I was asked to tutor the student, I accepted with little concern. My reasoning was that I've helped all my friends with papers at some point and I usually succeed in my own essay endeavors, so why should I worry about my first tutoring session?

---

[1]Stephanie's "felt sense" is a reference to Sondra Perl's essay, "Understanding Composing," from *College Composition and Communication* 31 (December 1980) 363–69.

I was knowledgeable about the writing center philosophy of letting the students help themselves. I knew that my job was to listen and address the text in terms of the assignment and higher-order concerns. Then I would slowly work my way down to things like grammar. I was not to mark on the paper, only question and lead the student to discover and interpret his or her own mistakes and shortcomings. I had observed only an hour of tutoring previously and it appeared simple enough. The question is, simple enough for what?

I soon discovered that it was simple enough to understand, but not simple enough to practice immediately. As the student I was tutoring began to read aloud, it occurred to me that not being able to read the essay myself was going to make concentrating difficult. I couldn't pick out many points to question her about. The paper was definitely not a disaster, but it did need some work. I missed some content in my determination to catch grammatical errors and found myself mentally scurrying for generic questions to ask in hopes that they would lead to more specific questions.

The assignment was the "changing your mind" paper.[2] I asked what she liked about the paper and what she wanted specific help with. She told me that she liked the topic of the paper (how a friend's tragic car accident helped her find God) and wanted help with grammar and "making it clearer." The clearer part I could handle. We discussed the "before the change" aspect of the paper. She had written well about "during the change" and "after the change," but really hadn't established herself before the incident. I think that she found this discussion helpful. Then we moved on to grammar.

We moved our chairs closer together and began to go through the paper page by page. She asked me a lot of questions like "Does this go here?" and "Can I put this comma outside the quotation marks?" This segment of the tutoring session really made me sweat. I noticed a few things that didn't look quite right, but I couldn't figure out if they were awkward or incorrect. I pointed them out to her and said I wasn't sure if it was incorrect and that she should check her handbook. She then asked a tricky question about whether she should put her own thoughts in quotes. I found some spots where quotation marks weren't necessary. She looked relieved and our time was up.

---

[2]All first-year students were working on this topic, based on Chapter 7 of *The Allyn and Bacon Guide to Writing* by John D. Ramage and John C. Bean. Here was the way this assignment was described by one instructor: "Write a brief autobiographical narrative shaped by contrary experiences or opposing tensions in which you tell the readers about a time when you changed your mind about something significant."

I went back to the main office, filled out the summary of our session and picked up a grammar handbook to double-check any advice I had given her. Everything looked okay except one of my quotation comments. It looked like she should have put quotes around one of the thought statements—where I thought quotes were unnecessary. I began to become really anxious. What did I tell her? Did I say something that was going to get her paper marked down?

I worried the whole walk home. Finally, when I reached my apartment, I couldn't stand it any longer and called information to get her telephone number. She was home and I told her that I had looked in the handbook and maybe she should take another glance at the one sentence. She thanked me for taking time to call and then we hung up. As I put the receiver down, I was overwhelmed with a feeling of incompetence.

For the past couple of weeks, I've been observing more tutoring sessions. I feel like I need it to gain more confidence. I know that my grammar in essays is often correct, but it has been a real struggle for me. I've learned that I can apply certain grammatical concepts correctly simply because I use them over and over. They fit my style of writing. What surprises me about tutoring is the number of grammatical conventions students use that I don't understand simply because I *don't* use them. There is a lot of variety at my disposal that I never really noticed until I started observing/tutoring at the writing center.

All of this information has started to move my own writing process. Nights like tonight and last night have been more challenging. I revised one of my papers as if I were in a tutoring session. Surprisingly, it was easy to look at my own work objectively. I found sections to question and rework. Tonight when I revised my philosophy paper, I discovered a sentence with a grammar mistake. I started to rearrange it into two correct sentences, when I realized that I was doing what I always did. I was reworking it into my grammar comfort zone. I decided that just this one time, I would expand my horizons. I got out my freshman grammar handbook and looked my sentence up. I'm proud to say that, earlier tonight, I used my first semicolon.

–Stephanie Wankum

Don't be afraid to take a handbook off the shelf and say, "Let's look this up." We have copies of the first-year students' required handbook in every tutoring office, to help them get the idea that they can use the handbook on their own and that they will find good things there. We also feel free to admit to writers that we don't know exactly what's wrong with a given sentence, but that we know it needs revision. Until you know more about grammar (and nothing will teach you about grammar the way tutoring does), it's good enough.

You might try this with other tutor trainees: In the tutor training course at Marquette, the trainees teach grammar to one another. We make up a list of common errors. Some of these errors are pretty simple, and we can feel comfortable just reading the rules for them. But some are very confusing, and it would help us help students if we knew more about how to punctuate conjunctive adverbs, when to use commas with restrictive and nonrestrictive elements, when to use "which" and when to use "that," when to put commas between coordinate adjectives. These terms take most of us way outside our grammar comfort zones, but if you teach one another, somehow, good learning takes place. We come to class with a stack of grammar handbooks, and groups of trainees look up these concepts in all of them. They decide on a topic and design a handout. Then, over several class days, they teach one another. Last year, for the rest of the semester, trainees joked about knowing what a conjunctive adverb was ("however," or "nevertheless," among others), but they were glad when they had to explain how to punctuate one. And the work with handbooks makes the trainees familiar and comfortable with them.

SELF-ASSESSMENT

After your first session is over, you can do some self-assessment. Sometimes you'll feel like Stephanie, full of doubts about parts of the session, and sometimes you'll feel like Caroline, happy to have helped. (And clearly, Stephanie helped, too, since the part of the session where they dealt with higher-order concerns went well; that would often be as far as the session got.)

After your first session is over, try to be as respectful to yourself as you have been to the writers you've worked with. You realize that sometimes when they are making mistakes, it means they are trying out new things, and they just simply have to have enough opportunities to try them out before they'll get them right. Sometimes when writers discover the beauty of the semicolon, for example, they overuse it and get it wrong. They'll get it right, if they have the right kind of feedback.

So you need the right kind of feedback, too. You need feedback from the writer, so don't hesitate to ask for it. "Did this session help you?" (And believe it: You'll know when *not* to ask that question.) Chances are the writer will grin and tell you, yes. Then you need to do your own self-assessment. Ask yourself these questions:

TUTORING SELF-ASSESSMENT QUESTIONS

1. What type of tutoring went on in the session? (Brainstorming, work on a first draft, final draft, or what?)
2. Was the writer able to articulate the kinds of help he or she needed before the session began? or during the session?
3. Did you and the writer establish a good rapport?

4. What is the proportion of tutor talk? What kind of talking did you do?
   - Interpretive paraphrase?
   - Directive questions?
   - Open-ended questions?
   - Advisory directives?
   - Content-clarifying questions?
   - Opposition-based questions?
   - Other? (What?)
5. Was the writer asking good questions of the text, too?
6. Did you ever find yourself interrupting the student, or did you listen and then wait a second before joining in?
7. Did you encourage and/or praise the writer's work?
8. Did you allow digressions when appropriate? Were you able to get the discussion back on track? Did you finish the session on time?
9. Was the writer critical of the instructor or the assignment? Grades? What kind of tone did you and the writer set for this discussion?
10. Did the writer try to get you to do the writing? How did you get around that?
11. Did the writer seem to be able to step outside the paper and analyze it (the structure, for example, or the audience or the purpose)? Did you model that kind of analysis?
12. Afterwards, did you help the writer to see what had gone on in the session? Did you ask what his or her plans were for moving the project forward?
13. What do you think the writer got out of the session?
14. What was most positive for you in the session?
15. What would you do differently if you had more time?[3]

Write some notes in your tutoring log (see the example at the end of Chapter 5). Seek out someone to discuss the session with. Talking it over will help you think productively about it.

Remember the sessions you observed, and remember that everyone, even the most seasoned veteran tutor, has awkward or poor sessions, encounters a writer who may have been made to come and doesn't want help, or wonders where to begin a session after listening to a seriously flawed paper. Recently, one of our veteran tutors was at his wits' end because a writer seemed indifferent, was shoving peanuts into her mouth while reading, and didn't really want to change her draft. Those sessions happen to everyone, once in a while. And if your first session has even one or two areas where you feel you helped the writer well, it will have been worth his or her while to be tutored.

---

[3]This list of questions was modified from a list developed by Peter Carino, "Posing Questions for Collaborative Evaluation of Audio Taped Tutorials," *The Writing Lab Newsletter* 14 (Sept. 1989) 11–13. Modifications were made with Jon Olson for "Tutor Training," *The Writing Center Resource Manual,"* ed. Bobbie Bayliss Silk, NWCA Press, 1998.

It may help to read Andy's account of having been tutored. He is one of our trainees who, as part of his training, was required to be tutored on a reflective paper.

Last Sunday, I was walking across campus, trying to think of a central idea around which to focus my reflection paper for this class, when I had a burst of inspiration. It was a windy day, and I saw the way the shadows of the tree branches danced on the ground as the wind blew through the leaves. I thought about how, in the Biblical story of creation, God separated light and dark on the first day. I thought of God's separation of light and dark as the simplest distinction between light and dark and a beginning. Interactions between light and dark have become infinitely more complex since the original separation. People have learned to control light and shadow and have used this knowledge to produce great works of art.

I saw the increasing complexity of interactions between light and dark as a great metaphor for learning how to be a writing center tutor. I thought that I could describe how our class began with the idea of nondirective tutoring as our light, separated from the darkness of directive tutoring, and that the idea would just snowball from there. I thought, "Great! Now that I have this killer metaphor, I can write this paper in an hour or two. Everything will just fall into place around this metaphor." This was a great relief to me because I had a busy week and knew I would not have much time to devote to writing this paper before getting tutored on it. I thought when I got tutored on the paper, I would impress the tutor with my incredible metaphor (maybe even make her reconsider the way she thought about tutoring), and she would help me with a few passages that were not clear. I would fix those sections in an hour or two on Thursday, in time to go out Thursday night.

I started writing my paper Tuesday night at midnight, and my tutoring session was the next morning. I worked until two and was really frustrated. The paper was not writing itself the way I thought that it would. I realized that I had a lot of thinking to do about what I actually thought about tutoring. I wasn't too worried, though. I still had my great metaphor that was going to make this paper work and wow my tutor. I could fill in more details about tutoring by Friday.

I went to the session the next morning and was pretty confident. Val was tutoring me, and I had observed her before. I told her before I read the paper that I had written it quickly late the night before, so it needed quite a bit of work. Then I began to read my paper. As I read it, my stomach began to get a bit queasy. I noticed that I described increasingly complex interactions of light and dark in my first paragraph. In the next paragraph, I described my reactions to learning about nondirective tutoring during the first week of class. I referred back to my metaphor vaguely in the last sentence of the paragraph. I then vaguely described the first tutoring session I had observed and, again, referred back to my metaphor in the last sentence of the paragraph. I thought, "God this paper sucks!" I knew I was going to admit there were a lot of problems in my paper, so I redefined my goals for the session. My goal became to save my metaphor. I finally finished reading the paper, not even really hearing what I read in the last couple of paragraphs.

Val asked me the standard question after I read my paper: "Now that you've read your paper what did you think of it?" I stumbled verbally around words for awhile before slowly stating, "I thought that my examples were really unclear. I have to put more concrete facts in my paper about what really happened in those sessions." Val had me reread the passages in which I described my reactions to things the class had discussed and tutoring sessions I had observed. She asked me about things that happened. I knew that she was drawing good material out of me for my paper, and I appreciated her doing this for me, but I was stunned to find that I was being tutored.

After we discussed passages, Val asked me what I was trying to accomplish by using my metaphor. I described to her what I explained in the first paragraphs of this paper. She asked me if I ever had said that in the paper. I reluctantly answered, "no."

I became more shocked the more things we talked about in my paper, and the more I realized I was being tutored in an actual nondirective session. I realized I was not prepared for the questions Val asked. I thought I asked myself these questions as I wrote, and that was enough. Despite what we learned in class, I thought tutoring was for less-developed writers who did not know how to ask themselves these questions while they were revising their own papers.

Finally, after I had described my metaphor and tried to tie it more closely to the details of the process of learning to become a tutor, Val asked me again why I was using this metaphor. I explained to her the great inspiration I had been blessed with the previous Sunday. Then she asked the question I was afraid to hear all session. "Do you think you're letting your metaphor control your writing?" I knew the answer. I knew it was. I had to admit that I had to get rid of my metaphor, or it would ruin my paper. I could not admit to her that I was going to give up my metaphor, so I quickly answered yes to her question and changed the subject. We talked a bit about things not related to my paper, and I left more than a little bit dazed by what I had just experienced.

Before the session, I was still quite skeptical about nondirective tutoring of writing. I had observed three sessions with freshman writers. The common factor I observed across sessions was that both the tutor and writer looked somewhat tired and frustrated by the end of the sessions. I questioned whether there was a more efficient, less-taxing way of helping people become good writers. I also did not know whether the students would improve their papers, because they did not leave with fixed papers. They left with "things to work on." I understood that there were things I realized about my writing during the session that I could not articulate and did not have to for the session to be successful.

Before Wednesday, I believed I knew enough about my own writing so that I would never need a real tutoring session. I expected to just go through the motions of being a tutee in a tutoring session. Experiencing a successful tutoring session as a tutee made me realize the true value of tutoring, and it was the most valuable experience I have had in learning to become a tutor. It was not easy for me to be tutored through a successful session. It was humbling and thought-provoking, but it was extremely helpful. When I finished my session, I felt like I had the look of fatigue on my face that I had seen on the faces of students when they were finished. I think now that the look was not a look of frustration because the session went poorly, but a look of realization that they had some further thinking to do about their writing, and that they may not get out until an hour later than they thought they would on Thursday because they were going to spend that time becoming better writers.

—*Andrew Helminiak*

HAVE I TALKED TOO MUCH?

We want to end this chapter by sharing some tips for talking and listening that Carol Kaufman, Trissa Luzzi, Libby Miles, and Christine Fox Volpe from the University of Rhode Island gathered from the Internet listserv WCenter (and generously allow us to reprint here). In your first sessions on your own, one of your main concerns will probably be, "Did I talk too much?" Here are some of the ways you might find out, and, more important, how you might counter the tendency to talk too much:

Techniques for Judging How Much Tutor Talk Is Too Much:

- If you are hoarse at the end of a shift, you are talking too much.
- Shoot for no more than 50% of the talking, unless the situation really warrants more.
- Tutors tape (audio or video) their own sessions and judge for themselves.
- Tutors observe one another and provide descriptive feedback.

Methods for Self-Monitoring Your Talk During a Session

Attitudinal Shifts for Tutors:

- Assume the role of the writer's audience, rather than the role of a writing "expert."

- Periodically ask yourself whether or not you are talking too much, just to raise your own level of awareness.

Behavioral Techniques for Turning the Session Over to the Writer:

- Ask the writer to read the paper aloud (rather than reading it aloud yourself) so that the writer gets comfortable using his or her own voice.
- Give the writer time and space to enact the revision principles you've discussed by leaving the tutoring space for a little while (get a handout, look something up, print something out, or just make up an excuse to leave the student alone a bit).
- If you are modeling in the session, do it once, then ask the writer to try the next one. Follow up by asking the writer to describe what he or she did.
- If the writer seems to want the tutor to do all the work (and talk), ask him or her to walk you through the paper, explaining what has been attempted with each paragraph.
- Ask follow-up questions such as "How else might you say this?" or "What do you think?" or "Tell me what you meant by that."
- Ask such descriptive meta-analysis questions as "What have you done when you've encountered this problem in the past?" or "What do you think your strengths are as a writer?" or "What kinds of comments do you hear about your writing?" or "What do you know about yourself as a writer?"
- Ask speculative questions such as "What would happen if...?" or "How do you think your teacher might respond to...?"
- Always offer multiple alternatives when modeling revisions or word choice for writers. Afterwards, ask the writer to make a choice and explain why a particular option was picked. See if he or she can add more to the list of possibilities.
- When you ask questions, wait for the answer. Be patient. When you think you've waited long enough, wait that amount of time again. In other words, wait twice as long as you think you need to before stepping back in. You'll probably find that the writer was really thinking during those moments, and not just staring into space.
- Make sure the writer gets the last word. At the end of the session, ask the student to summarize what happened. You may need to prompt with such questions as "What writing issues emerged as we worked together?" Next, follow up by asking the writer to describe the strategies you developed together for attacking or sidestepping the problem. Finally, ask what the writer plans to do next to continue the revision. The idea here is for the writer to have the last word.
- Build regular reflective moments into your day (between sessions, before tutoring for a shift, after a couple of sessions, on a day off) to stop and ask "What else might I do to encourage the writer to talk more?"

9

READING IN THE WRITING CENTER

We start this chapter by asking you to consider the following question: What do you do when you read?

Your answer might focus on the "perfect" environment that you seek out when you read or perhaps on the specific strategies you use to engage with a text. Here's how students in the peer tutoring course at Marquette responded to the question: From Sheri:

> When I am reading for class, for starters I make sure that I have all of my reading supplies. These include my glasses, a highlighter, pencil, blue pen, notebook paper, dictionary, and a quiet place to read, which has a desk or table (It also has to be cold!). Before I read for class or for research purposes I always look over chapter headings or bold print words and then formulate questions based on these. When I do this it helps me to become more interested in the text I am reading because I am now looking for answers.
>
> Also, if there are study guide questions, I will look them over so that I have a basic idea of what to look for. I will then read the text all the way through, find the answers to my questions, and underline all of the study guide answers in pencil.
>
> When I read for fun it's a whole other story! I always take off my shoes and sit on the floor/ground or in a very comfortable chair. I always prefer to read in natural light and preferably fresh air. I just read and relax and totally immerse myself in the story or article or whatever!

From Sara:

> When I read for class, I always have a pen or pencil in hand to write down observations, underline important info, and so forth. When I was in high

school, I had a teacher who wanted us to keep logs of what we read, and when I read something that is especially important, I try to do that. Most of the time I have too much reading to do that very often though. Also, I prefer to read for class in a quiet place, but I'm pretty good at focusing even when there is a lot of noise. I rode the bus to school in junior high and high school for over two hours a day, and I learned to concentrate and do homework in the middle of the craziness of that environment.

I liked the idea about taking a nap before reading boring material. A lot of times I'll be reading something and get so sleepy. If that happens, I usually just let myself nap for awhile, but it might help if I went into the reading fresh.

From Aesha:

Usually when I read, I need a quiet spot so that I can concentrate. My bedroom does not count, because there is a bed and a chance that I might find myself on it with my book as a pillow. I also need to form a visual image of whatever it is I am reading; otherwise, it won't make sense to me. I've tried writing marginal notes and underlining, but I'm not too consistent with that (something I need to work on). With the really difficult stuff, I have to read out loud. It helps me to concentrate and it keeps my mind from wandering too much. One thing that I have found that I have liked is reading with someone. My boyfriend reads aloud with me on occasion. When we do this, we each have to summarize the portion that we read to the person who is listening. This helps with my listening skills, too.

From Susan:

I'm what some people call a close-reader. It's reminiscent of the Seinfeld "close-talker"—but not exactly the same.... I sit with my pen in my hand and plod along, reading every last word, circling, underlining, and writing little notes to myself. Evelyn Wood I am not. Sometimes I wonder about the time invested in this style of reading. I mean, I've been known to write marginal comments in *newspapers!* So much of what I read, I'll never read again. But, then, something happens like the little surprise exercise that we did in class today, and I'm darn glad that I have my thoughts all gathered in scribbles at the end of the page!

These responses might seem quite familiar to you; after all, if you have achieved success as a writer, it's quite likely that you're also a successful reader. Hopefully, you enjoy reading, find yourself catching chapters of paperbacks while waiting for the bus or between classes, or regularly comb used bookstores in search of treasures. Many writers you'll meet in the writing center, however, won't be either as skilled readers or as fond of engaging with their texts. In fact, reading and writing are inextricably linked, intertwined in ways that make it difficult to determine whether a student's difficulty with a writing task is a problem with his or her reading or writing or both. As a writing center tutor, you'll encounter many clients who are writing from sources, and those sources span the disciplines and genres—from literature and poetry, to essays and editorials, to textbooks, to newspaper articles, to advertisements. And in the service of helping students become more skilled writers, you'll need to know some of what they are facing as readers. How can you help them become more strategic readers, developing control and flexibility, just as was your goal for them as writers? How can you work with writers who are reading texts far outside your major? And how can you avoid being positioned as a content expert when writers are reading texts with which you're familiar, in a sense avoiding being positioned as an editor/interpreter rather than as a tutor? These are some of the questions we address in this chapter on reading in the writing center.

DEVELOPING STRATEGIC READERS

In looking at the research on the relationship between reading and writing, Robert Tierney and Timothy Shanahan come to the following conclusion: "What has emerged from this research is a consistent finding: Writing prompts readers to engage in the thoughtful exploration of issues, whether it be in the context of studying science, social studies, or literature" (268).

As the movements to incorporate writing across the curriculum (WAC) or writing in the disciplines (WID) flourish, more and more students come to our writing centers having written in response to something they are reading. At times this writing is simply to make sense of what they are reading; at others, it's to analyze or evaluate, and still at other times it could be to present that reading as a background for the writer's own research. As you surely know from your life as a student, the kind of writing tasks you'll engage with will be varied, and this variation has much to do with the kinds of texts you are reading. Ultimately, as a writing center tutor, you'll be encountering writers who are grappling with texts. At times, you'll be frustrated because the dilemma isn't a problem with the writer's processes for writing or even command of mechanical issues (though some reading problems sometimes manifest themselves this way); instead, the problem is with a writer's understanding of what he has read. "He just isn't getting it," you think. "How can I help?"

One source of help is to understand some of the processes of reading. When you considered the question "What do you do when you read?" you might have thought of specific strategies you used to engage with your texts. Now consider the question, "What do you do when you read something you don't understand?" Do you picture the writer and try to figure out what his or her intention was? Do you make associations with the text? Do you gloss the text, making notes in the margins, asking questions, underlining and highlighting what you believe to be important? You probably have a variety of strategies that you have found essential to your reading. Here's a list of strategies that workshop participants at Bristol Community College's 12th Annual Conference on the Teaching of Writing came up with in response to "What do you do when you read something you don't understand?"

- Reread
- Look up words
- Take notes on content
- Write summaries
- Question oneself
- Take breaks
- Change environment
- Just keep going
- Check understanding word-by-word
- Imagine the writer
- Discuss with another
- Get frustrated
- Break sentences down into manageable parts
- Read out loud
- Give up
- Speed up
- Ignore it

Unlike this rich variety of strategies, poor readers have a limited repertoire and little conscious control and flexibility of the strategies they do possess. For example, one of the frequent strategies poor readers employ is simply to reread something they don't understand. However, rereading won't be of much help if the vocabulary is unclear or if there's background information that the reader is missing or if the text is structured in a way that's unfamiliar to the reader.

In our chapter on the writing process, we stressed the idea of metacognition or awareness of one's own learning process. When it comes to reading, metacognition is equally, if not more, important. In fact, one concept we introduced—levels of strategic knowledge—comes from research on reading. Scott Paris, Margerie Lipson, and Karen Wixson believe that the goal for readers is to develop three levels of strategic or metacognitive knowledge: (1) declarative knowledge or knowing what strategies are available;

(2) procedural knowledge or knowing how to use a strategy; and (3) conditional knowledge or knowing why and when to use a strategy. Successful readers have a strategic repertoire that they consciously control; poor readers often do not.

Reading researcher Ruth Garner views a reader's metacognitive knowledge as having three components: (1) knowledge of self or of one's own abilities; (2) knowledge of the task itself; and (3) knowledge about specific strategies to approach the reading task. Each of these components plays an important role in determining whether readers will have successful encounters with their texts. As a reader, your goal is to develop control and flexibility.

So what does this mean for you as a writing tutor? Well, your goal as a reading tutor is to help develop writers' control and flexibility of their reading processes. There are several ways you can do that:

- Ask the writers you're working with about their reading strategies. In posing this question, you help them first become aware of their thought processes, and then you can comment upon the appropriateness of that strategy or suggest refinements.
- Talk about the reading strategies that *you* find successful. Show the writer a text you've marked up, explaining why you made the comments you did and how your notes, underlining, or highlighting are intended to help you understand and respond to the text.
- Model the reading strategies that work for you. Read a text aloud, vocalizing the thoughts that are occurring to you as you read. In this way, you are making your thinking visible for the writer. Or co-read a passage with the writer, comparing your thoughts, comments, and strategies with his or hers.

In addition to these methods, you can help writers learn how to use three common strategies of successful readers: (1) looking up words they don't understand, (2) identifying the text's main ideas, and (3) asking questions about what will happen next in the reading (Cole and Griffin). For the first strategy, you might show a writer how to use a dictionary (not everyone will know how to do this well). For the second, you can use the writing of summaries as a way of increasing the writer's reading comprehension. Behrens and Rosen break summary writing down into several useful procedures:

- Read the text carefully first.
- Reread the text, dividing it into sections or "stages of thought." Then label these sections with a few descriptive words.
- Write one-sentence summaries of each stage of thought.
- Write a one- or two-sentence summary of the entire text (the writer's thesis for the summary).
- Write the summary itself.

Have writers summarize their text by following these procedures and then you can tutor them on the summary itself. Thus, you'll be helping them with their reading *and* their writing.

For the strategy of asking questions about what will happen to the text, we recommend you demonstrate for writers a procedure known as SQ3R (Vacca and Vacca). This acronym stands for:

Survey: Have the writer preview the text to get a general sense of what it's about, making note of subject headings, indentations, underlining, and boldface or other means of placing emphasis on certain parts of the text. Ask the writer how this text is like or unlike others she's read before and have her make guesses about what she will read based on the title, headings, subject matter, assignment, and the like.

Question: Based on the survey, have the writer ask questions (and write those down) that she feels the text will answer. Help model some of these questions if the writer is stuck.

Read: Have the writer read the text (and reading aloud will give you an idea if her difficulties are a matter of vocabulary), searching for answers raised in the previous step.

Recite: In this step, the writer reads aloud or writes down the answers to the preview questions. You might try and answer some of her questions as well and then compare your responses to hers.

Review: Have the writer reread certain portions of the text in order to reach clarity on the answers to the questions raised.

Certainly, these strategies won't necessarily work for everyone. Once again, as a tutor, you need to be flexible about what to use in specific situations. What is important is that you make writers more aware of their reading strengths and weaknesses and that you help them rely on their strengths and overcome their weaknesses.

Overall, your job isn't to explain the meaning of a text to a writer who is confused; instead, you want to help the writer discover that meaning, not just of that particular text but of future readings. When Stephen North said, "Our job is to help students become better writers," he certainly could have added, "and better readers, too."

EXAMPLES OF READING IN THE WRITING CENTER

We want to give you some examples from actual tutoring sessions that show just how complicated it can be to deal with reading in the writing center. The tutor's and writer's familiarity with the reading itself and the writer's understanding of the assignment and the task, among other factors, can greatly affect what happens in writing center sessions. Your overall goal should be to help the student become a better reader and writer, but as the following examples show, at times this goal is easier to accomplish than at others.

Example 1—Co-constructing Confusion

In our first example, the tutor is a graduate student in sociology, one who has a professed dislike for working with writers on "literary analysis." The writer is an undergraduate in first-year composition whose task is to write an essay after reading *Howard's End*. Here's how the session begins:

Tutor: Okay, why don't you tell me a little something about the assignment.

Writer: I'm supposed to read this, *Howard's End*, the first three chapters. And I'm supposed to figure out…there's like two parts to this. The first part where there are the letters. That's Chapter 1. Then Chapter 2 and Chapter 3 is like the actual story. And then we're supposed to say how the letters that were written about some of the characters…well, the character I did was Charles Wilcox. We're supposed to see how the letters in the first chapter show what kind of person he is and demonstrate what kind of person he is in the second and third chapters.

Tutor: Okay, so it's basically describing Wilcox, right, in the context of the novel?

Writer: Yeah.

Tutor: Okay. So why don't you tell me a little something about what you've written.

Writer: This guy, Charles Wilcox, is basically like a really masculine person. He's really kind of authoritative in a way. He's like his father, similar to his father. I wrote how he's similar to his father. There's stuff inside the story, and I just read that and relate it to the second chapter.

Tutor: Okay. I'm sort of digging back now because I remember seeing this movie. Did you see this movie?

Writer: I haven't seen the movie, and I haven't read the book except those chapters.

Tutor: Yeah, it's a good movie. Okay.

If red flags are waving in your tutor-mind's eye, you're developing strong sensibilities for detecting trouble. The tutor here is "ignorant" in that he's unfamiliar with the book (though he's seen the movie) and is thus dependent upon the writer to "teach" him the book's content (or at least the content of the chapters in question). But the writer's brief recapitulation of what he's written ("There's stuff inside the story, and I just read that and relate it to the second chapter.") sounds awfully vague, the first sign that he perhaps didn't understand what he had read well enough to write a character analysis.

Later in this session, the tutor is reading the writer's paper aloud (indicated by all capital letters in the transcript) but comes to a passage that he finds confusing:

Tutor: HELEN SAYS THAT THIS MORNING IS "NOT LIFE BUT A PLAY." SHE WAS AMUSED TO WATCH THE WILCOXES THAT TUESDAY MORNING. THE WILCOXES SEEMED COMICAL BECAUSE ALL OF THEM ARE ILL. MRS. WILCOX WAS WATERING THE GARDENS...Okay, I don't really get that.

Student: Yeah.

Tutor: Why is that comical and amusing?

Student: The ones on the hill are the ones that are working out. Like, Evie was working out on like a tree or something, and both the Wilcoxes have been playing croquet or something, and Helen was amused.

Tutor: Oh, I see. Okay, so you need to put that in to show what's amusing, right? And Mrs. Wilcox is not ill, and she's wandering the garden. Is she aware of the others or is she just more self-absorbed?

Student: It seems like she's more self-absorbed. She's just paying attention to herself and the flowers and just watching them at 7 a.m. in the morning.

Tutor: So what you're going to want to do is to interpret this to show why would they seem comical. This sounds strange when you say, "They seem comical because they're ill." You don't normally say that about someone who's ill but if they are, you know, they're not seriously ill right but they're just like constantly sneezing.

Student: Right, I should say they're sickly?

Tutor: If you say they're sick, it's the same thing but...

Student: I can't seem to get it in my head how to reword it. Can you think of a word?

Tutor: The thing to try to do is to try to look at this family, the Wilcoxes, from Helen's point of view, right? Because Helen is probably seeing things about them that they don't even see themselves, right?...To try to get into her head in a sense. And that's what literary analysis often is. It's getting into the mind of the character. And in this case it's getting into the mind of Helen and seeing why she'd be interested in this family and these characters.

Student: So I should write "the Wilcoxes seem comical to Helen because they're all so active, uh, and they're all sick." That seems, I don't know...

Tutor: [Sighs loudly] Does that make sense? [long pause] Maybe just do this then, all right? "She was amused to watch the Wilcoxes that Tuesday morning. The Wilcoxes seemed somehow comical to her." Just take this out. [loud crossing out sounds] This is not helping this at all. [more sounds of crossing out]

Student: Okay.

In this excerpt, the focus is on one word, *ill,* but it's indicative of the tutor struggling to understand the writer's presentation of these characters. The tutor offers a possible way of approaching the task, couching his advice in disciplinary terms ("And that's what literary analysis often is. It's getting into the mind of the character."). However, the writer continues to focus on the rewording of a small part, ultimately leading the tutor to a frustrated crossing out of the writer's work. It's hard to imagine that either participant emerged from this session feeling that his or her goals were met.

Example 2—Crossing the Line

In some sessions, you will know well the reading that the writer is trying to understand or you'll have a strong interpretation of that text's meaning. In these instances, the temptation is strong to simply dole out your understanding or interpretation to the writer, who will eagerly accept your "words of wisdom." If you feel this temptation, ask yourself if it is in the service of developing the writer. Sure, you might have had teachers in the past who stood up in front of the room and announced the "correct" meaning of a story or essay, but did you learn anything in those instances (anything positive, that is)? And is the meaning of texts so fixed and stable that we can simply dump it from our heads into the writer's?

In the following example, we believe the tutor, a graduate student in applied linguistics, crossed the line. The undergraduate writer here has the task of responding to a short quote from Henry David Thoreau's *Walden.* The tutor is first reading aloud from the writer's text (indicated by all capital letters) and then reads part of the Thoreau quote before she begins asking the writer questions:

Tutor: THOREAU EXPLAINS THE SIMILARITIES THAT HE SEES BETWEEN ANTS AND HUMANS. And then he writes "WATCHED A COUPLE

THAT WERE FAST LOCKED IN EACH OTHER'S EMBRACES IN A LITTLE SUNNY VALLEY AMID THE CHIPS." What does this mean?

Writer: Like, you know, on a tree, the little leaves that are at the bottom.

Tutor: Okay.

Writer: They were underneath it.

Tutor: Okay, why does he say it like that. Why doesn't he say "on that frightful day with the pouring rain"?

Writer: Because he wants you to see that everything was hunky dory, everything was just perfect.

Tutor: Or, at least he wants to make it seem, maybe not perfect but…

Writer: There's no conflict.

Tutor: Okay, or, what else? That's the way things go. You fight. Survival of the fittest, right? That's life. The sun is shining. Those ants are amid the chips. Why are you shaking your head.

Writer: I don't know how you come up with these things.

Tutor: Does it make sense though?

Writer: Yeah, it doesn't matter whether people are still…, you know, is that what you're trying to say?

Tutor: Well, I want you to see it.

Notice that the tutor is primarily trying to lead the writer to *her* interpretation by asking questions (evidence perhaps that questions aren't necessarily a nondirective form of tutoring). The writer is certainly aware of this, asking "Is that what you're trying to say?" after she somewhat unsuccessfully puts the tutor's words into her own. Here's one more passage from later in the session, an even more directive attempt by the tutor to have the writer guess the interpretation that the tutor sees:

Tutor: So now you have "NOW AT NOON DAY PREPARED TO FIGHT TILL THE SUN WENT DOWN OR LIFE WENT OUT." What does that mean? You're an expert now, so you have to tell me.

Writer: That I'd talk about how they're going to fight until the end of the day or till one person there is a victor or they're going to fight until the fight is over.

Tutor: Okay, excellent. Now you've gotten that far, now we're going to push it even further. Why noon? Why not 1 or 3 or 5 or 7 o'clock? Why did he pick noon?

Writer: I don't know.

Tutor: When you look at a clock, noon's up here. What does noon also represent?

Writer: 12?

Tutor: Good answer. What else does 12 represent? Or let me be more specific, what does 12 o'clock represent?

Writer: p.m.

Tutor: Or?

Writer: The night.

Tutor: What else?

Writer: When is the sun going to set in a few hours.

Tutor: Okay, actually at 12 p.m. what is it going to do?

Writer: The sun is going to go down in a few hours.

Tutor: Okay, it seems like the sun has been setting at 3 in the afternoon, but we'll just say, okay, we're going to go around the clock, around the clock 11:59, what is it now?

Writer: One minute to 12.

Tutor: Okay, now it's 12. Is it…?

Writer: It's the day.

Tutor: Right so what 12 o'clock is that?

Writer: What do you mean?

Tutor: It's not p.m. it's…

Writer: a.m.

Tutor: Right, so the sun is going to rise. Twelve is kind of that point where the day changes, right?

Writer: Okay.

Tutor: Does that make sense?

Writer: That makes sense, but I can't see how it relates.

This extended lesson in clock reading once again has the tutor leading the student toward the tutor's interpretation of the passage. In its fits and starts, its reinforcing phrases by the tutor ("Okay," "Good answer"), it's difficult to characterize what seems to be going on here as learning. Rather than engaging the writer in a discussion of her interpretation of the passage and an analysis of the strategies she's using to make that interpretation, the tutor instead pulls the student ever closer to guessing what's in the tutor's head. It would seem far more efficient (though certainly not a positive model of tutoring) for the tutor to tell the writer her interpretation up front and cut out all of the guessing! In many ways this technique is an example of the power of expectation, as we presented in Chapter 4. Perhaps the tutor expects the writer to have the same interpretation as she does—and that the tutor's interpretation of the passage's meaning is the "right" one! We urge you to be careful if you find yourself practicing similar techniques and ask yourself if you are serving the best interests of the writer.

Example 3—Coconstructing Meaning

Our third example focuses on the writer's reading of poetry. However, in this instance the tutor and the writer were much more closely aligned than in the previous examples. Both are familiar with the task of literary analysis, the tutor as a graduate English student and the writer as an undergraduate English major. They have also met several times before, and the writer comes to this session primarily to talk about how to begin his analysis before he's done any writing. Here's how this session starts:

Writer: I have to write a five-page paper on sonnet 144.

Tutor: Okay, now tell me what they want you to do. Do they give you any direction or none at all?

Writer: He gives no direction at all. He said "4 to 5 pages."

Tutor: So he said, what, just analyze the sonnet?

Writer: Yeah.

Tutor: Okay. And can you talk about anything?

Writer: Yeah.

Tutor: Okay, so that's really open-ended. Okay, so where do we start?

Writer: It's kind of scary. I mean I can pick any sonnet. I chose 144.

Tutor: Okay, I guess, good and that was going to be my next question. Why did you choose it? And start from that. What strikes you about it, either in terms of content or style? Ideally you'll talk about both. See it's such an open-ended assignment, I'm wondering if you want to talk about, like, a thematic thing and talk about content or if you want to do some sort of stylistic analysis.

In this opening, the tutor first clarifies the assignment and then immediately shares her knowledge of the task of poetry analysis. Notice that her language isn't delivered as commands; instead, she uses phrases such as "I'm wondering if you want to" and "I think you should," indicating that the writer must ultimately make these decisions.

This session proceeds as a coreading of this particular sonnet and a coconstruction of its interpretation. Quite often, the tutor is simply reading lines from the sonnet and thinking aloud as she models her reading and analysis processes:

Tutor: "And whether that my angel be turned fiend suspect I may, yet not directly tell." I'd have to mull on that line for a bit.

Writer: Yeah.

Tutor: "…suspect I may yet not directly tell." I think I get it. "But being both from me, both to each friend, I guess one angel in another's hell." I'd mull on that line, too.

Writer: Yeah.

Tutor: What does that mean "I guess one angel in another's hell."? "Yet this shall I ne'er know now, but live in doubt, to my bad angel fire my good one out."

Writer: To me it sounds like…

Tutor: Why don't we just put down, [she writes] talk about what intrigued you about it.

Writer: And it's kind of like the crux of his struggle with the sonnet. I mean in his sonnets because this is the one where…

Tutor: Good, talk about that, relate it to the other sonnets.

Writer: He is more drawn to the male lover throughout the whole series of the sonnets, but there's that side of him that gets the woman, too, and here the woman takes his male lover away, so he loses both, and now he has nothing. I think that it's just kind of the high and the low.

In this exchange, the tutor moves from a close reading that makes her thinking "visible," to supporting the student's analysis ("Good, talk about that, relate it to the other sonnets.") from the perspective of an "insider" to the discipline. These kinds of interactions are not merely an expert *telling* a novice the "correct" interpretation of this sonnet. Instead, the tutor models the ways of thinking about poetry, asks questions of the student, and gives commentary about those questions to reveal the foundation upon which analysis—and close reading—is built.

These three examples come from the kinds of tasks writers in English classes might face (though not all of the tutors had expertise as writers of these sorts of tasks). In the writing center you'll work with writers who are reading many more sorts of texts, some of which you might be familiar with and many with which you won't. If you are familiar with the specific discipline, as in our third example, you'll have opportunity to model and discuss the ways your discipline organizes and presents knowledge (for example, the presentation of primary research in the sciences). But if you and the writer do not share disciplines, no matter. As tutor, your goal is for the writer to teach *you* the content of the reading material. And you can help the writer do that by sharing what you know about successful reading and by helping writers become strategic readers—in control of specific reading strategies and flexible about when and how to use those strategies. There's a good chance that your sessions might not even address the writer's paper itself, but that's what subsequent appointments can be for. Your *immediate* concern, in a somewhat ironic sense, is the writer's long-term development. The strategies, habits, and thought processes of successful readers are all a vital part of that development.

10

WORKING WITH ESL WRITERS

We have often found that a large source of anxiety for new tutors surrounds the work they will do with ESL writers. "Will my knowledge of grammatical terms and rules be adequate?" they wonder. "Will my session get bogged down into line-by-line identification and correction of error?" they fear. "Will I emerge from a session spent and bleary eyed, hoping to find someone to talk about 'big ideas' and not the minutia of English mechanics?" they ask. "Will I be pushed into the role of editor instead of being a tutor?" they fear. Certainly, these concerns are understandable; after all, many of you have had little contact up to this point with ESL writers.

In this chapter we want to address your concerns by confronting several misguided ideas surrounding ESL writers. One of the first comes from the label "ESL" or "English as a Second Language." More likely, many of the non-native English speaking writers you'll work with have English as a third or fourth language or grew up in bilingual (or trilingual) households. Thus, for the purposes of this chapter we'll use the acronym NNS for non-native English speakers.

Along with countering some persistent myths, we want to give you practical advice for working with NNS writers, and call on the thoughts and words of Marquette's tutor trainees to help you on your path to becoming secure in your abilities as a tutor. In many ways it's odd to dedicate a single chapter to NNS writers—a student population whom you'll generally tutor just as you do native English writers! Nevertheless, the worries that you might have are ones shared by many beginning tutors, and we'll attempt to address those concerns.

MYTH #1—NNS WRITERS HAVE WEAK COMMAND OF STANDARD WRITTEN ENGLISH

Like many generalizations, this one doesn't hold up well in the face of concrete evidence. As classroom teachers we know that some of our strongest and most gifted writers did not speak or write English as their first language. In the writing center, we see a wide range of preparation and skill among NNS writers. Certainly some had a great deal of work to do to master certain aspects of English grammar and usage, particularly those aspects that do not exist or are in very different forms in their native languages (for instance, articles and subject-verb-object sentence order for many Japanese and Korean speakers). And many simply haven't had extended exposure to idioms and culturally specific usage.

However, even those NNS students with a weak grasp of mechanics are working to express and share meaning and have meaningful things to say. Your work with them will often be some of the most rewarding sessions you'll conduct as you guide them to express their ideas in clear and coherent ways. As Sara, a tutor trainee at Marquette wrote, working with NNS writers is "a great way to meet a person from a different culture with a different take on the world." And Angela added, "I think the great part of working with [NNS] students is that they are so much happier when they get it. There is such a contagious enthusiasm when students who struggle more than average have a breakthrough."

MYTH #2—NNS WRITERS THINK DIFFERENTLY FROM NATIVE ENGLISH SPEAKERS

One of the more influential pieces of early research on NNS writers was done by Robert Kaplan, and in his research he described culturally based rhetorical patterns, ones he expressed in graphic form (and thus his article is often referred to as "the doodles article"!). For instance, in many Western countries, linear and direct argument is favored. In Asian countries, much of the writing is indirect and is sensitive to the writer's status vis-à-vis his audience, and in some Arabic countries, the rhetorical approach is more circular, approaching the main point only after a certain amount of preliminary negotiation. While these broad generalities, based on examinations of texts written in various cultures, have some truth, they are unfortunately extended to the idea that a pattern in writing necessarily means a pattern in thinking. However, consider the impression you would make if everything you wrote consisted of the five-paragraph essay; would you want people to think that was the way you actually *thought* about each topic? Formats and rhetorical styles are certainly products of cultures and conventions we often are only barely aware of and value highly without really knowing why. But don't pigeonhole an NNS writer into a particular mode of thinking because of the rhetorical style to which he or she is accustomed. In fact, some of those NNS writers might be eager to break away from those at-times rigid structures. As one Japanese writer told us, "Before I came [to the United States],

I tried to make my papers difficult; I tried to get some difficult phrase, you know, some old proverb across.... So very philosophical…but now I think it's a waste of time."

Nevertheless, we don't want to dismiss the role that cultural practices and expectations will play in your sessions with NNS writers, as we discussed in Chapter 4. Some writers will come from cultures that have gender expectations that you don't share (for example, men who are uncomfortable being tutored by a woman), some will have very different notions than you do about personal space (and will sit closer or farther away than is comfortable for you), some will position you as an authority in ways that you don't expect and will be surprised either by your informality or whether you prefer to keep that tutoring door open or closed. And, as we have seen repeatedly, many NNS writers will have a very different view on plagiarism than is probably the policy at your school; notions of intellectual property and attribution are quite culturally specific. However, given all of these differences, you shouldn't assume that NNS writers have cultural expectations that are fixed. NNS writers will often be open to learning about our expectations for matters ranging from personal space to gender roles to plagiarism. What is most important is to try to open up these issues for discussion. In terms of tutor and writer behavior, talk about what tutor and writer responsibilities should be in a session. For cultural issues that have to do with what's in a writer's text, discuss your expectations for what accurate use of sources should look like and why you believe this to be the case. You will surely encounter sessions where a "clash of cultures" seems to be interfering with the work of tutoring; however, if you open up these topics for discussion and examination, you will be helping NNS writers a great deal.

MYTH #3—NNS WRITERS COME TO THE WRITING CENTER TO GET THEIR "GRAMMAR CHECKED"

Several parts of this myth need scrutiny. First, the request from an NNS student for you to "check my grammar" doesn't necessarily mean she wants line-by-line editing or for you to proofread her work. It's often a matter of vocabulary that results in such requests. In our experience, "check my grammar" can mean a whole range of requests, from "give me feedback on structure and organization," to "react as a reader to my argument," to "help me interpret this assignment." Many students, native and non-native speakers, simply aren't well versed in the vocabulary of writing tutoring. However, for many, the association between correcting grammar and tutoring writing is pervasive. But as a tutor, you'll have the opportunity to teach NNS writers that language of tutoring, and what once was a "grammar check" can next time be a request to "tell me if my evidence supports my thesis."

Furthermore, in the previous schooling of many NNS writers, "good" writing has often meant "correct" writing, and a focus on grammar is simply transferring what many of their instructors have requested. We know too well the instructor who just sends NNS students to the writing center, telling students, "Have the writing center fix that paper and come back to me so that I can grade your content." So often you won't be dealing only with a writer's request for a "grammar check," but also a classroom instructor's. As Aesha, a Marquette tutor trainee said, "For [NNS] students, grammar *is* a higher-order concern. It is emphasized in class, they are downgraded for improper use, and it is hard to understand and remember all the funny little rules about it. In fact, most native students wouldn't be able to recite all the rules about commas; we just use them."

To counter this myth, we recommend that you start a session by asking about the assignment and the class. If you do so, you will be able to uncover a great deal about who determined the writer's agenda. It's also essential that you be patient, working carefully to clarify the NNS writer's needs. Here's an observation from Paul, a Marquette peer tutor, that demonstrates what we mean:

> I found that the session went very smoothly because both Maria and the tutee were patient. I saw that it was important for the tutor to make sure the student understood what she was explaining. I also saw the importance of the tutee questioning anything confusing. But this is something I feel should be in any session we observe/tutor. Patience and understanding are two key factors to tutoring anyone. Just because someone does not use English as their native tongue should not change that.

Finally, we offer some fine strategies from Niki, another peer tutor: "Ask [NNS] students questions in order for us to better understand them: 'What do you feel like you have the most trouble with?' 'What was a concern that your professor brought up in your last paper?' 'What is difficult for you about writing this paper?' I think if we dig more in that direction, we can understand what an [NNS] student feels like when they are having problems with their work."

MYTH #4—NNS WRITERS JUST NEED MORE OF THE BASICS BEFORE THEY CAN MOVE ON TO MORE SUBSTANTIAL WRITING TASKS

This is a persistent and dangerous myth, one that surrounds not just NNS writers, but is a myth for any writer whose previous schooling left him or her underprepared for the level now attained, as composition researcher

Mike Rose has shown. Many NNS writers have had years and years of "the basics," which usually means grammar drill-and-practice worksheets. Whether in their native countries or in [NNS] classes in the American public school system, approaches to remediating underprepared students are little "cure" for the "problem." Instead, they offer students sentence work that's removed from any meaningful context. And NNS students often master that sentence work quite readily, easily conjugating those verbs and matching up pronouns and antecedents. However, once they're called upon to write—to express themselves in meaningful ways—cultural and cognitive overload can result. Writing is hard, complex work. Filling in blanks in a workbook is often not.

Myth #4 also assumes a writer's development to be based upon a "building-block" approach, that is, first master sentences, then paragraphs, then controlled essays. But think about how you would react if you were restricted to only a sentence to express a complex idea or to persuade someone to agree with a position about which you feel strongly. Or imagine that you only had a paragraph to do that expression or persuasion. NNS writers need opportunities to work with complex forms as befitting their complex ideas, not to plug thesis and evidence into five-paragraph templates. In the writing center, you'll have great opportunities to enable NNS writers to transcend their previous schooling and express themselves in sophisticated ways.

MYTH #5—I NEED TO "CLEAN UP" THE GRAMMAR IN NNS WRITERS' PAPERS BEFORE WE CAN GET TO HIGHER-ORDER CONCERNS

Closely related to Myth #4 and the idea of a building-block approach to writing development, this myth contradicts the advice we gave you on HOCs (higher-order concerns) and LOCs (later-order concerns) in Chapter 3. NNS writers will still be seeking feedback on meaning, structure, and evidence; unlike some native English writers, they will also be seeking feedback and instruction on English grammar and usage. However, we urge you not to give in to the easy inclination to tackle LOCs before HOCs. And we have found that NNS writers, while concerned about grammar and usage, will also be concerned about higher-order matters. They might need to make a second or third appointment to have all of their concerns addressed, but most will be amenable to that suggestion. Even in sessions where writers report that they need help just with grammar and usage, our approach is first to talk about the assignment, the writers' approach to the assignment, and the gist of what the writers are trying to say in their papers. These conversations in and of themselves will often lead to the writers expressing concern about higher-order matters and dictate a less LOC-centered session.

In the following example, note how the tutor acknowledges the writer's request for a language-level focus in the session (one essentially dictated by the classroom instructor), but still takes the time to ask about higher-order matters, one that he can discuss first with the writer and then focus on when examining her paper:

Tutor: Let's see, you're a sophomore in [liberal arts]. What can I do for you?

Writer: I am writing this paper for [an international relations] class.

Tutor: Okay.

Writer: The teacher's got us all freaked out about it already.

Tutor: That explains it.

Writer: He read over this yesterday for me. The contents is basically all set as far as all that. I just basically need to know if my grammar is...

Tutor: The language-level stuff.

Writer: Exactly. I think the organization is fine; I don't think there's a problem with that because he read over it, and he thinks it's okay, and he doesn't want to do it again, I guess.

Tutor: Okay, give me the sort of two-sentence overview of what the paper is about. Give me some context, or at least what the assignment is.

Quite often, even if NNS writers have a language-centered agenda, we ask them to read their whole texts aloud. This approach not only gives NNS writers practice in English pronunciation (and many will ask you how to pronounce certain words), but gives you a chance to assess the text as a whole and address those higher-order concerns that you feel need scrutiny. You'll find yourself saying things like, "Yes, there were some problems I heard with subject-verb agreement, but since we might end up changing those sections anyway, let me first ask you about what you were trying to say in this section of your paper."

However, you will also encounter some writers whose problems with English pronunciation and reading are severe enough to interfere with your session: They'll be struggling and you won't be able to understand. When you have a student like that, we recommend you feel out the situation by asking him or her to read the assignment sheet aloud or just the opening paragraph. If you feel the work of the session will be better accomplished if *you* read the text aloud, try that technique, and ask the writers to stop you when they want to mark something for revision. You can read over the errors, as they would, and come back to them later so that you can focus on content and support first.

MYTH #6—I NEED TO BE WELL VERSED IN THE TERMINOLOGY OF ENGLISH GRAMMAR AND USAGE IF I'M TO TUTOR NNS WRITERS

Well, this is one myth that has some element of truth. We do advise you to spend time with your favorite grammar handbook and become familiar with explanations to common grammatical problems. This is because most of the NNS writers you encounter will have quite complete grasps of terminology; they'll know their parts of speech and the rules of sentence construction. Endless filling in of those drill-and-practice worksheets imparted many of the rules and terms. In fact, we probably have gained much of our knowledge of English grammar from the inquiries of NNS writers about the difference between "might" and "may" or "that" and "which." Rather than spout these answers off the tops of our heads and act as living grammar handbooks, we co-consulted those handbooks with NNS writers, reading together those sometimes arcane explanations and examples and applying that knowledge to NNS writers' texts.

Nevertheless, it is worth your while to be able to ask an NNS writer to identify the subject and the verb of a sentence to check if they agree in number or to ask if a word is functioning like a noun or an adjective. Grammar terminology can give you and the NNS writer a common vocabulary and greatly help your tutoring. But we want to reinforce that you don't have to be the source of all grammar knowledge; as we said, many NNS students will have quite advanced knowledge of the "rules." As Jamie, a Marquette trainee, said, "Most [NNS] students will not need someone to tell them all the answers. From talking with tutors, and through our staff meetings, I've gathered that by merely asking questions about problematic areas in a paper, a tutor can focus an [NNS] student to analyze the problem area(s), and most times the student will be able to see and correct the error(s)."

MYTH #7—SO MUCH OF THE ENGLISH LANGUAGE IS IDIOMATIC AND THUS CAN NEVER BE TAUGHT

Certainly a great deal of what native speakers take for granted comes from growing up in an English-speaking culture. Our immersion in the English language makes it second nature to use the correct preposition or to know that we can "talk about" but not "discuss about" some topic. And even what might seem like rules in English often have bewildering exceptions. For instance, we know that we use the definite article "the" before concrete nouns, particularly those that are "old information" or have already appeared in the text ("A boy approached. The boy seemed friendly enough."). However, how come we use the definite article before certain bodies of water and not others (e.g., for "the Caspian Sea," "the Mississippi River," and "the Atlantic Ocean," but not for "Lake Ontario" or "Walden Pond")?

Many NNS writers will not be versed in these idioms or will use vocabulary in ways that defy our "native" connotations (one student who offered to "eradicate" the blackboard is an example). However, they will also be looking toward you, if you are a native speaker of English, to help them with idioms, to share some of your cultural knowledge. As Sarah, one of our trainees observed, "If she didn't know that it was a mistake in the first place, then she couldn't identify it on her own." It's important for you to identify those problems in an NNS writer's text that deal with some fairly hard and fast rules of English usage and those that demand native competency. For the latter, you'll often need to let the NNS writer in on those "little secrets" that we hold dear.

MYTH #8—I'LL NEED TO BE A MUCH MORE DIRECTIVE TUTOR WITH NNS WRITERS

This is a myth we hear fairly often from less-experienced tutors. And we're not entirely sure what it means to be "more directive." We hope it doesn't mean making changes for the writer or "cleaning" texts while the writer passively sits by, nodding politely. What we think this myth means is that beginning tutors find themselves in an unfamiliar position when working with NNS writers, particularly in those instances when the focus is on language-level concerns. We suspect that many new tutors are coming to learn that, when focusing on language, the approach of allowing the writer to spot his or her own errors doesn't always work with NNS writers; it's difficult to apply knowledge that one doesn't necessarily have in the first place.

When you think of the processes of error correction, you can imagine that it consists of at least three stages: (1) spotting the error; (2) identifying the appropriate fix; and (3) applying that fix. Many writers, NNS and native speakers, will be quite skilled in #2 and #3, but for a variety of reasons won't be so strong in spotting their own errors (this is the reason that it's easier to proofread someone else's paper than your own). For instance, you'll probably work with writers who tell you that they always have problems with comma splices and who can engage you in an extensive discussion of how they can use a semicolon to separate those independent clauses or pop in a coordinating conjunction after the comma or break those clauses into two sentences with a full stop between them. However, when you look at their papers, you'll find a whole host of comma splices! In these cases, you can perform what composition researchers call a "governing" function, but what we like to refer to as "the power of the index finger." You will find that all it takes for NNS writers to supply a correction is for you to point with your index finger at the problem. Often, you won't even need to say anything like "comma splice" or "subject-verb agreement." Your isolation on a problem will often be enough for the writer to focus in on the error and then call up his or her knowledge of how to fix that error.

Generally, for approaching the language-level concerns of NNS writers (after you've dealt with higher-order concerns), we urge you to keep in mind the advice we gave in Chapter 3 when we talked about error analysis. Often, NNS writers will have patterns of errors, as well as fairly complete logic behind the error. It is your task to identify those patterns and prioritize. Don't overwhelm the writer by focusing on many different errors at once; instead, rely on single passes through a paper or a paragraph with a fairly specific focus. For instance, if you see that the writer has a problem with subject-verb agreement, focus in on a single paragraph first and ask the writer why he or she conjugated the verbs in a specific way. Then, you can point out some of the instances where the subjects and verb didn't agree and explain why. You'll often find that the writer will make the correction himself or herself. Next, have the writer apply this knowledge to his or her text, examining the next paragraph and noting subject-verb agreement errors and making corrections where needed.

Research in error analysis has shown that NNS writers can more easily identify problems with verbs, rather than something for which there are many idiomatic exceptions, such as articles. In the case of articles, it's also important that you ask the writer for the logic behind his or her choices. By asking about this reasoning, you'll often find that the writer has misapplied a rule or created a rule where one doesn't necessarily exist. However, with so many exceptions to the rules, when it comes to articles, the ear plays a large role, and correct use of articles seems to come only with time.

Obviously, this is slow (and some feel tedious) work, but what you are doing is teaching the writer, not correcting texts or claiming ownership. You can then perform this same strategy with one or two more errors, if time permits. If not, sign the writer up for another session with you in which you can work on additional aspects of his or her language (signing the writer up with another tutor isn't particularly efficient since you've established a relationship and have broken important ground). Sara, a Marquette tutor trainee, reinforces our point based on her observation of NNS sessions: "I think that it would benefit [NNS] students a lot if they would find a tutor that they were comfortable with and see that person on a regular basis throughout the semester. Part of the frustration I felt when I observed was that it seemed like we had only just begun when the hour was over."

We want to end this chapter by offering some reminders of how to work with NNS writers. Keep in mind that:

- HOCs (higher-order concerns) still come first.
- Error analysis is essential and can be a slow process. It's important that you be patient.

- Ask the writer about the logic behind an error in order to understand fully why the mistake occurred.
- Most NNS writers can figure out their own verb tenses and agreement, particularly if you begin by pointing to the specific problem.
- If NNS writers need direct or indirect articles or American idioms, we can give them those. This is not dishonest—they simply have nowhere else to get this information.
- Remember to point out those occasions when they get their grammar and usage right; NNS writers can learn from those models.
- If they use good sentence structure or are effective with such things as subordination and coordination, tell them so.
- We might not finish in the allotted time, so urge the NNS writer to make multiple appointments.
- Try to get the writer to keep working with the same tutor.
- Urge NNS writers to do as much reading as they can and to make American friends.

11

DISCOURSE ANALYSIS

In tutoring sessions, you can experience powerful acts of teaching and learning (and one of the wonderful things about tutoring is that it can be either participant—tutor or writer—who is doing the learning or the teaching). The fact that this learning comes about through language, through talk about such things as words, ideas, and assignments, makes studying the language of a tutorial one of the best ways to acquire an understanding of what happens and why.

Carefully studying your sessions can also transcend one of the many contrasts in tutoring writing—tutor versus researcher. A persistent belief is that research is done by a certain group of people and that tutoring is done by another group, and never the twain shall meet. We instead believe that everyone involved in writing center work is a researcher—from directors, to tutors, to writers. The most important purpose of this research is to better understand what we do so that we can then improve upon it. However, we also generate knowledge as researchers. Analyzing patterns in one's own sessions, then comparing that analysis with other tutors, noting similarities and differences, and working toward what's generally true and what's specific to your tutoring—these are the ways that we create knowledge that the writing center field as a whole values (and you can then share this knowledge in the form of conference presentations or articles). Thus, we believe that tutors *are* researchers.

In this chapter, we hope to equip you with the means you'll need to analyze your tutorials. We'll introduce some of the basics of discourse analysis, helping you to break down a complicated task into manageable chunks. By applying some of these techniques, you will be well equipped to analyze and learn from your tutoring: You'll be "doing" research!

TUTORIAL INTERACTION AS DISCOURSE

At Marquette, a regular part of the training is to have tutors tape-record one of their sessions (first gaining the writer's permission, of course) and then analyze what they see occurring. This analysis can be challenging, however. How can you make sense of what you hear? How do you know if something "worked" or not? How can you best understand the way you and the writer communicated?

Writing center researchers have devoted a considerable amount of time trying to answer these questions and to characterize just what tutorial interaction or discourse is like (e.g., Davis et al.; MacDonald; Walker and Elias). Is it a conversation akin to what peers would have with each other? Is it more like the interaction between students and classroom teachers? Some combination or unique hybrid? Addressing these questions is important for many reasons. For instance, if we want to characterize a session as "effective," we need to figure out what effectiveness looks like. Certainly, a session that primarily featured a tutor doing all of the talking wouldn't be effective in most people's views, but most sessions are much more complex than that (in fact, Walker and Elias found that who dominates the talk was not a factor in how effective tutor and writer perceived their sessions to be). Examining the features of the interaction lets us make some headway toward understanding—and thus improving upon—what we do.

Once we start looking at the interaction, we need to use some techniques to help sort things out. For example, imagine that you're reading a transcribed tape of your session and want to find out how "controlling" you were. You could do several things: You could count up the number of words both you and the writer spoke and see who said more (assuming that dominating the interaction is a measure of control). Or you could try to characterize the function of what you said to the writer—did you ask questions? Make statements? Issue orders? Or you could examine how you followed up each time the writer said something—did you cut the writer off before he could complete his statement or question? Did you offer the writer a paraphrase of what he said or asked in order to verify your understanding?

These particular ways of examining the transcript are just a few of many methods. Most important, what you look for depends upon the questions you pose. In other words, in the examples above, we were mainly trying to determine what "control" looks like. You might also ask, "Were the questions I asked open-ended, and how did the writer answer them?" "How did I approach the teaching of grammar?" "How did I make my goals and responsibilities known to the writer and my expectations for his responsibilities in the session?" Over all, when analyzing your sessions, you need to come to the analysis with fairly specific goals. Perhaps these goals will come from your training class or perhaps from your own personal analysis of what you want your tutoring to be like.

To give you an idea of one tutor's analysis of her session, we turn to the following excerpt that involved Paige, a graduate student in Theology. The writer in this session was analyzing an article on agricultural methods of developing nations.

Writer: This sounds weird.... It doesn't seem right, where here "is this a need for" and down here "is this a necessity" because it changes from the 18th century, which is like this, to the 20th century, which is this. I mean, is that too close together?

Paige: You mean close together because you don't talk about the 19th century or close together because you use that phrase?

Writer: No, because it's talking about...yeah, because it's like this is saying, "it's needed," and this is saying, "it's not needed," and it's just such a quick...I mean does it make any difference?

Paige: Well, if you want because you're...

Writer: I mean I could make a separate sentence about it but...

Paige: You have made a separate sentence. If what you're trying to do is contrast these two, you could contrast it with "however" or "on the other hand" or something like that that would show this is different.

Writer: Do you think that's really needed or am I being really particular?

Paige: It couldn't hurt just to go ahead and emphasize the difference between the two eras.

Writer: Okay let's see...so should I add in the sentence or just restructure this part of it?

Paige: You can do either; it's up to you.

Writer: Okay.

Note that the writer is focusing on a particular phrase, essentially seeking Paige's correction; Paige, however, deflects making the correction outright, but instead investigates why the writer feels the correction is needed. When Paige does offer a possible change, strengthening a contrast with a transition word, she still leaves the final choice up to the writer with: "You can do either; it's up to you."

In an interview, Paige listened to this sequence and then commented upon what she was hearing: "Typical pastoral counseling techniques coming out." Expanding on this technique, Paige described it as "laissez-faire tutoring" and added:

The student is saying, "Tell me what to do." You can picture them coming in here and pulling a knife and demanding to know what to do.

"What do you think would happen if you put your knife away?" It is nuts. Sometimes they get totally frustrated because they want the answer, and you tell them they can find the answer. There are many different answers and many options and not necessarily a "best" option, so you need to find the option that's going to fit what you want to do.

Thus, this brief sequence reveals Paige's underlying philosophy of tutoring—to reveal potential options for the writer but to have the writer decide what will ultimately work best. And for Paige, this philosophy emerges from her experience in pastoral counseling.

Will all brief sequences from your sessions be as indicative of your approach and experience? Probably not, but analyzing your sessions will begin to make clear just what it is you're doing and how you might change some of your tutoring techniques.

THE SPEAKING MODEL OF DISCOURSE ANALYSIS

For our first more-structured method of analyzing your tutorials, we need to introduce some terminology from sociolinguistics. Dell Hymes has described several concepts that are helpful in thinking about tutor/writer interaction, particularly in uncovering the underlying social "rules" that govern our behavior. The first of those is a "Speech Situation" or "situations associated with (or marked by the absence of) speech" (56). Hymes gives the examples of ceremonies, meals, or fights. Speech situations do not have broad rules that govern them, but are a broad boundary under which we can examine the next term—"speech events." In Hymes' words, a speech event refers to "activities, or aspects of activities, that are directly governed by rules or norms for the use of speech" (56).

So how do these terms apply to tutoring? Well, you can consider the whole range of tutor (or teacher) interaction as speech situations and within that broad class, many types of speech events: classroom lectures, class discussions, student-teacher conferences, and, of course, writing center sessions. Each of these has rules that participants follow, sometimes making those rules explicit but usually not (and think about those times when someone violated the social rules and how people reacted: someone talking during a lecture, one person dominating a group discussion, a writer showing a bad attitude during your tutoring session). Hymes' interest is in uncovering these social rules that we largely adhere to unconsciously. By exposing these rules, we can begin to see the logic behind our behavior and particularly why miscommunication can occur. Did that writer really have a bad attitude or did he simply have an entirely different sense of the social rules of tutoring than you did?

To perform this analysis, Hymes introduces the acronym SPEAKING. We'll briefly define each of these terms and then give an example.

S—Setting and Scene: For tutoring sessions, the setting is, of course, where the session is held, but as you think about this aspect of the analysis, think about particulars of your locale: Are you and the writer sitting across from each other or next to each other? Are you at a rectangular table, on a couch, or around a circular table? Do you have harsh fluorescent lighting or incandescent lamps? Each of these components plays a role in creating an atmosphere and sending strong messages about the rules to be played in the session itself.

P—Participants: Most often this will be you and the writer (and perhaps an observer), but certainly, the classroom teacher can also be a very "visible" participant.

E—End: Sociolinguist Peter Farb describes that "when people speak, they do so in the expectation that a certain outcome—an exchange of information, the obtaining of something, an expression of their status, and so on—will result" (38). For tutoring writing, both you and the writer come to a session with certain goals or ends, both long and short term. Try to identify these ends as well as you can when analyzing your sessions.

A—Act Sequence: This term refers to the actual dialogue that you will be analyzing. As we'll show in the example, start with something short and seemingly routine, such as the opening of a session. It is in the ordinariness that you can often find the greatest unstated expectations and agendas.

K—Key: This term refers to a what is often the mood of the interaction. Some examples of key are ironic or serious or playful. Often nonverbal clues can give you an indication of an interaction's key, such as whether the participants laugh or smile or how closely they are sitting.

I—Instrumentalities: While we'll assume that your sessions are conducted in English, the specific vernacular will probably vary depending upon the relationship you feel with the writer—formal, informal, or specific vernaculars such as Black English. Thus, instrumentalities refers to the "forms of speech" (Hymes, 63) that are used.

N—Norms: This term refers to the rules that apply in a given speech event. We usually don't shout out questions during a lecture; we expect to get our turn during a conversation; when we ask a question, we expect the other participant to offer an answer. Sequences within tutoring sessions will often have separate norms, for example openings of sessions, where it's usually the tutor who starts things off with a question, and closings of sessions, where the writer is often expected to give some indication of the usefulness of what occurred.

G—Genre: Hymes refers to genre as "categories such as poem, myth, tale, proverb, riddle, curse, prayer, oration, lecture, commercial, form letter, editorial, etc." (65). Certainly, different sequences within tutoring sessions will resemble different genres, for example, a lecture or counseling session or a conversation between peers.

Now that we've outlined the SPEAKING model, we want to show you how it can be applied to a sequence from an actual session. We'll use an excerpt that comes from the very beginning of a session and walk you through the analysis. Much of the "inside knowledge" of our analysis comes from interviews with the tutor and writer involved, but you should be able to perform an analysis without that additional insight.

Setting

The writing center where this session occurred is housed in an Academic Resource Center that's part of a large, private urban university in the Northeast. The room where tutoring occurs is small, windowless with a rectangular table and a couple of orange-covered straight-backed chairs. Tutors and writers usually sit side-by-side, choose to leave the door open or closed, and face a bulletin board with the writing center rules posted (e.g., "We do not proofread!"), as well as articles for tutors to read on various aspects of tutoring writing.

Participants

The tutor in this excerpt is Paige, the graduate student in Theology we introduced you to earlier. The writer is Leslie, a senior international relations major. Leslie has never been to the writing center before and is coming this time at the urging of her classroom teacher. Leslie is a bit frustrated by her grades in this class and figures that visiting the writing center might send the message to her instructor that she'll "do what it takes" to improve her grade. Thus, in many ways, Leslie's instructor is also a participant in this exchange (and figures prominently in the Act below).

Ends

For Paige, any tutoring session should result in the writer emerging better equipped herself to go about her writing tasks. In a more immediate sense, she also wants the writer's paper to improve, but the improvement should largely be as a result of what the writer does, not necessarily what Paige might do. In the beginning of a session, Paige wants to get an idea of the writer's goals and begin to formulate a plan as to how she might help the writer achieve those goals.

Leslie, as we said above, is largely driven in this session by a desire to improve her grade in her international relations course. However, as a major in that field, Leslie also wants to master the material and communicate the discipline's ideas in a way that shows she "belongs." After graduation, she plans on joining the Peace Corps, and thus has a strong commitment to her major and field.

Act

The following exchange opens the session:

Paige: So what class are we working on today?

Leslie: EE 510

Paige: Oh, my goodness. I think my roommate was in this class at one point. Who's the teacher?

Leslie: Professor R_____.

Paige: Mm, hmm.

Leslie: Great.

Paige: [says something unintelligible]

Leslie: Okay, well this is the assignment I'm working on, and I have typed, printed this out and I brought the…I don't know how this works, so you should tell me how it works, and then I'll just follow your lead because I've never been here before. Actually Professor R_____ says he sends his students here all the time. So he thinks this is a good thing.

Paige: Okay. As soon as I have a chance to look over this we can look at your paper. In the meantime, could you fill this out for me? [hands her the writing center new-client form]

Leslie: Sure.

Paige: Because you've never been here before. So it's project number 2?

Leslie: Project number 2, and then this, and here's the article that I read, this, for the assignment.

Paige: Okay.

Key

In the opening of this sequence, you can see the informal, peer-to-peer bond that Paige creates by showing some knowledge of the class and instructor ("Oh, my goodness. I think my roommate was in this class at one point. Who's the teacher?"). Also, note how Leslie reveals that she's never been to the writing center before and asks Paige to "tell me how it works"; she wants an explicit understanding of the "rules of interaction." Thus, the key here is friendly and cooperative, while at the same time quite focused on the task at hand; they set ground rules and get right down to business.

Instrumentalities

The English here is fairly informal (e.g., "oh, my goodness") and in many ways resembles a conversation between peers. Note that Leslie asks Paige to take the lead in structuring this session ("I'll just follow your lead."), deferring to her expertise and showing that while the language used might be informal, the participants' roles aren't necessarily equal.

Norms

While Leslie acknowledges that she's never been to the writing center before, she does come to this session with some sense of the "rules" in that she defers to Paige's expertise to structure the session, as we note above, and Leslie also comes quite prepared with an assignment sheet, the article she was responding to, as well as her paper itself. Note also that Leslie invokes her classroom teacher's endorsement of the writing center ("Professor R_____ says he sends his students here all the time, so he thinks this is a good thing."), thus endorsing Paige's work herself and affirming Paige's expertise as a tutor. So the norms in this sequence are that Paige will set an agenda and help Leslie as the writing center has done for Professor R_____'s other students, and that Leslie will come to this session prepared.

Genre

In the broadest sense, the genre is a tutoring session. In a more narrow sense, the genre is the opening to a tutoring session, one where tutor and writer establish agendas, create or maintain relationships, and indicate what their specific responsibilities will be.

This analysis covers just a snippet of a tutoring session, but reveals a great deal of the underlying meaning. As you apply the SPEAKING model to your own sessions, you'll gain insight into not only the ways you act to achieve your goals, but also the ways in which writers respond to your actions. By looking deeply at even a small part of your tutoring, you can reveal the essential factors that often mean success or failure.

FEEDBACK SEQUENCES

Our second structured method of analysis addresses one of the challenges of analyzing tutorial discourse: deciding upon what comprises a "unit" of analysis. You could just look at questions and answers as several researchers have done in examining teacher-student interaction in the classroom (e.g., Mehan). In classrooms, a typical pattern of interaction is for the teacher to ask a question or initiate a sequence ("What's the capital of Mississippi?"), then for students to offer an answer in response—perhaps with some teacher prodding ("Biloxi?" says Jonny.), and finally for the teacher to evaluate that response ("No, Jonny, that's not correct.") This sequence is known as the IRE (initiation, response, evaluation) pattern of classroom discourse, one quite dominant in classrooms (Cazden). Also, notice how teacher-centered and controlling this pattern can be as the teacher plays a "guess-what's-in-my-head" game with her students.

Several researchers (e.g., MacDonald, Davis et al.) have applied this framework to their examination of writing center sessions, and it is a useful one to consider yourself, particularly if you believe that asking questions isn't necessarily directive. However, questions and answers are only a part of the ways that tutors and writers will interact. For the others, we need some way of setting a boundary and describing a unit, which we can then analyze. By closely examining these units, you can learn a great deal about your approach to tutoring and the writer's reactions to your approach. For this purpose, we'll use a concept we call a *feedback sequence.*

In our study of tutoring, we often see how a writer seeks the tutor's feedback on how best to proceed with the text, whether this advice is on a word, paragraph, or whole-text level. Thus, most tutoring sessions can be seen as chains of requests for feedback. Some are started by writers, some by tutors, and some by the ever-present but invisible classroom teacher. Some focus on small bits of text and others on paragraphs, pages, or whole essays. And still others are more process-oriented and focus on the writer's approach to his or her paper. Whatever the focus and whoever begins the sequence, either the tutor or writer closes the sequence by giving an evaluation or offering a correction, and then the other participant indicates it's time to move on to the next section of text or writing problem.

In many ways, entire tutoring sessions can be seen as one large feedback sequence, particularly in terms of how writers often start sessions with agenda-setting statements, such as "I wanted you to give me an idea whether or not my paper makes sense." Certainly, in the ideal case, a tutor doesn't simply say, "Yeah, this paper is fine," and end the session there. Instead, we urge our tutors to turn the evaluation back onto the writer, sometimes saying such things as, "Well, tell me what it is you're trying to say in your paper, and I'll tell you what I understood after you've read it aloud." Nevertheless, because most of the writers you'll encounter come in with a specific paper for which they're seeking specific feedback, you'll find yourself engaged in many rounds of evaluation and, oftentimes, correction as you point out some feature of the writer's text that doesn't work for you or for the writer. To help you identify these units in your own sessions, we next offer several examples of feedback sequences drawn from our research.

As we noted, either writer or tutor starts a feedback sequence, seeking some sort of reply from the other participant, and then the sequence is closed when the person who starts the sequence indicates it's time to move on to another concern. In the following example, the writer begins the sequence, one focused on her requests for evaluation of her whole paper. Once she receives a response from the tutor, she follows up with some commentary, in a sense reaffirming her initial request.

Writer: So like what do you think? I mean, I guess if I changed it around, do you think the paper has hope?

Tutor: Yeah, definitely. I like your format.

Writer: I like people to be hard on me.

Queries about specific chunks of text are common subjects for feedback sequences. In the following example, the writer seeks a paragraph-level evaluation on his application to law school:

Writer: Do you think this is all right, this paragraph, to leave in there?

Tutor: That's up to you.

Writer: Is it too personal? Again it said personal statement and I'm thinking they might want to know a little bit more about me other than my experiences, maybe to give them a little bit of a sense of who I am.

Common feedback sequences are those started by writers seeking the "right" word or a grammar/usage correction. In the following example, the tutor has just suggested a correction that would include the word "thus." Note that this sequence lasts more than just a single turn as the writer continues to inquire about wording until he seems satisfied:

Writer: When do you use "thus" normally?

Tutor: When you're concluding. Right? You're giving premises; thus, you have a conclusion.

Writer: But does it start a sentence or does it have to be in the middle of a sentence or it doesn't really matter?

Tutor: It doesn't matter. It's not a word that requires you to have it only in one place.

Writer: Is "thus" like a form of another word?

Tutor: No. It's its own word.

Writer: So it's a word itself. Okay.

In the above examples, it was the writers who started the sequence, directly seeking some evaluation of their texts. However, as a tutor, you will also begin these sequences, offering unsolicited feedback. This advice can range from suggested words to ideas for reorganizing text to tips on potential topics for a writer's text. At times, the sequence can veer closely to the classroom technique of "guess what's in my head," as in the following example where the writer is working on a paper on "Traumatic Brain Injury" or TBI:

Tutor: When you say something like traumatic brain injury, what do you suppose you need to do for your reader?

Writer: Define TBI?

Tutor: Yup. What is it? Right? So where do you think we could put that?

Writer: I'd put it in the first paragraph?

Tutor: Okay you can talk about what it is, and then you're going to talk about the problems, introduce the problems and what this paper's about. How about the second paragraph?

Writer: Okay. The definition, wait, want me to tell you about the definition in the second paragraph?

Tutor: Yeah, just like the general idea.

In the best of circumstances, your feedback will be more of a shared effort between you and the writer. While you might start a sequence, the writer will use that opportunity to start a sequence of his or her own and take some role in the correction of the text. In the following example, the writer has been reading aloud his text when the tutor stops him:

Tutor: Okay, it's a tiny, tiny thing…with "led" you just need a preposition with that, "led…"

Writer: "to"?

Tutor: Yes, exactly, "led to opportunistic feelings."

Writer: Do I need "the Middle East and the West" or I don't need the article?

Tutor: Oh, actually, yes, you do, I didn't notice it. Sure, yeah, "the West," exactly.

Finally, at times, it won't necessarily be you or the writer who begins a sequence of feedback; it will be the omnipresent classroom teacher, the ultimate evaluator of the texts in most writing center sessions. In the example below, the writer initiates the sequence, but it is in response to a criticism by the instructor, who is simply referred to with the pronoun "she":

Writer: Yeah, but I want to cross out some stuff because on my last paper that she gave back, she made a comment on the back that I don't have to summarize what the book is about. I should just stick to analyzing. So I was thinking, should I cross out this first paragraph?

Tutor: Okay, let's see. Okay, does this have anything to do directly with what you want to talk about?

Writer: No, just this part right here has something to do with it.

Tutor: This second half right? So why don't, just for now, why don't we just say that we can cut this out.

Writer: Okay.

Overall, a tutoring session is made up of many feedback sequences that often overlap. The language that tutors and writers use to start, participate in, and close these sequences lends much evidence toward understanding the responsibilities they assume in a tutoring session and the responsibilities they expect the person sitting across the table from them to assume. Do you believe that feedback on a writer's text should be triggered by the tutor's views of what works, the writer's stated agenda, the classroom teacher's stated criteria, or some combination of these influences? Examining feedback sequences in your sessions can reveal not merely your beliefs, but the specifics of your practice.

In an even larger way, the feedback sequence as a unit of analysis also holds promise in our understanding the underlying processes of learning in a writing center session. Some researchers believe that the "conversation" between writers and tutors is an explicit dialogue that, eventually, will become an internalized dialogue as writers develop their writing skills (Flynn). If this is true, then your feedback sequences might be the overt structure of this dialogue. In other words, if writers are learning how to think about their writing based upon the conversations we have with them in writing center sessions, then our examination of those conversations can reveal the issues and challenges of learning to write in college and how writers learn to overcome them.

Whatever method you use to analyze the discourse of your sessions, you will be contributing to improving your practice, as well as gaining insight that you can share with your fellow tutors or with the large writing center community. Tutors *are* researchers, and our hope is that this chapter has given you some ways of taking on that identity.

12

ON-LINE TUTORING

We write this chapter knowing perfectly well that technology and its rapid changes can make current devices obsolete as we move in the direction of videoconferencing and perhaps some undreamed-of choices. So we're not going to focus much on the technology; rather we'll talk mostly about the pedagogy, that is, the methods of teaching and learning that go on in electronic conferences, because we believe that the learning should come first and should not be driven by the technology.

We've done on-line tutoring in a number of contexts, with nuclear power plant employees, with adult learners enrolled in a weekend degree program, and with graduate students who can't schedule a regular appointment. We've even tutored our faculty colleagues ("Would you please look at the first sentence in this editorial I'm writing? Dr. Krause said it sounds a little pompous. What do you think?"). We've also tutored an entire class of advanced placement students about thirty miles away as a sort of experiment.

Most of our conferences have been fairly low-tech (asynchronous e-mail exchanges) for several reasons: E-mail is easy and reliable to use. It's easy to attach files to an e-mail message, and it's easy to distinguish the writer's text from the tutor's questions or comments. (The writer's text can have a > symbol at the start of each line.) E-mail allows the tutor plenty of time to formulate good questions. And e-mail allows the tutor to reply to the writer when it's convenient, or even from home, if that works. However, the higher-tech environments such as MOOs and chat rooms are becoming increasingly reliable and free of the lags that made them undesirable just a year ago, and with the real-time conferencing they allow, we can come closer to the f2f session, and the dialogue that real-time conferences allow.

ENCOUNTERING EXPECTATIONS

We did some research with a group of the writers who used our services, and we learned a bit about what they expected from us. We had gone to some lengths to let them know in advance what to expect from their tutoring sessions, but they still experienced some frustration that we did not immediately work on "grammar," as they referred to issues of correctness. They felt frustrated when we worked on higher-order concerns first.

They also felt threatened at first by all of our questions. In spite of the fact that we sent them messages saying, "We'll ask you some questions *for your consideration*," they felt that our questions had the force of commands. So we had to look for ways to ask questions that didn't sound like orders. Still, this sort of thing can happen in f2f conferences as well.

These writers we worked with took to e-mail conventions pretty easily, but in a paper presented at the Midwest Writing Center Association meeting, Erin Smith points out that we may need to teach some writers the conventions of e-mail. It has its own genre, she argues, and its conventions involve informal speech, tolerance of error, lots of joking around. (Some of the writers we surveyed joked around with us but didn't like it if we joked back.) She suggests sending writers an annotated sample or two of an e-conference. Something like that could easily be posted on a website.

ON-LINE TUTORING HOW-TO

In addition to sharing our experiences with on-line tutoring we wanted to give you some general guidelines. First, some real basics. No writing center that we know of allows writers to drop off their drafts and come back for comments. We involve writers in the revision process, make them part of the dialogue about writing in hopes that they will not only produce a better text but become better writers. We want on-line tutoring to offer the same benefits to writers. So we're still going to concentrate on higher-order concerns before later-order ones. And we're going to follow the same guidelines, as much as possible, that we've laid out in this book for f2f tutoring.

RESPOND QUICKLY

Don't let a message sit and sit. The writer has deadlines and won't be logged on nonstop, so try to reply to messages as soon as possible. Your director will have worked out with you some method of logging your time for these sessions.

ESTABLISHING A FRIENDLY TONE

When you respond to a request for on-line tutoring, it's possible, depending on the circumstances, that you'll be dealing with someone who thinks he is consulting an automated style checker. You'll want to reply with some kind of introduction of yourself as a tutor, and some kind of statement about what the session might consist of, or what you expect of the writer. Be friendly but avoid joking around. As we described above, the writer might not know how to take that.

ESTABLISHING THE CONTEXT

Even though it will slow the process down, ask the writer about the assignment, about her goals for the paper, her purpose, her audience, and about her writing concerns. You could conceivably receive an argumentative paper that's very well written for an assignment that calls for a narrative or an explanation. Just as in f2f tutoring, it's really important to know the writer's context and assignment.

READING THE TEXT

Will you be working either in a synchronous or an asynchronous system? If you are not on-line at the same time as the writer, you'll have time to read the paper and formulate a response. Make your reply personal with some kind of friendly introduction. The following example of Stacie's session sets a good, friendly tone and tells Kate what to expect. (This was a second exchange. In the first, she and Stacie introduced themselves.)

> Stacie (the tutor):
> Hi Kate! It looks like the second try worked. Isn't it interesting how technology that is supposed to help us makes things frustrating at times.:) In fact, this is my second attempt at commenting on your draft. My first attempt was totally lost when my computer froze up. (oh bother.) Just a little overview of how this is going to work. Lines of your draft are marked with "<" brackets. I'll be breaking in and asking questions and making comments. I like to use ** as tricks to highlight my comments. I'll be making lots of comments—don't panic or think that your draft is bad. There are just areas that need clarification. I'll try to give suggestions on the introduction and conclusion, as you ask.

HOCS BEFORE LOCS

Stick to higher-order concerns first and don't be tempted to react to sentence-level concerns or grammar problems—these may improve in subsequent drafts. Begin with something positive about the paper. Then comment on how well the paper meets the assignment, mention whether the paragraphs have adequate support or development, and ask unanswered questions the text raises for you. It's still possible to use questions to help the writer develop better papers. We usually resend the paper back to the writer with comments interlaced between paragraphs in a format that looks like the following exchange between Jenn, the tutor, and Kate, the writer:

> The writer's text:
> >The Witch and the Minister
> >Nathaniel Hawthorne's solemn "tale of human frailty and sorrow,"
> >The Scarlet Letter, is flavored with the cackle of witches and the
> >mystery of black magic. (46) Hawthorne adds the superstitious
> >elements to The Scarlet Letter with Mistress Hibbins. However,
> >Mistress Hibbins is not simply an incidental character in the novel.
> >Hawthorne uses her as the personification of Arthur Dimmesdale's
> >secret, guilty sin.
>
> Jenn (the tutor):
> ***I really like your opening sentence! It really draws the reader into your essay. Do the comments you make about Mistress Hibbins constitute your thesis statement? Are the final two sentences your argument/thesis? If so, how could you expand on these ideas a little more? As a reader, I'm not really sure what direction your paper is taking. I'd like to hear a little bit more about Mistress Hibbins.

As you probably noticed, Jenn did not comment on the placement of the period in the citation. She stuck with textual comments and questions. And she gave a reader response: "I'm not really sure what direction your paper is taking. I'd like to hear a little bit more about Mistress Hibbins."

There are some pros and cons to interlacing tutor questions, as Jenn did above, into the writer's text. You'll have to decide what works best for you.

Advantages	*Disadvantages*
Interlaced comments might encourage the writer to reread the paper as she looks for comments. This would take the place of reading aloud in a face-to-face session.	Interlaced comments intrude into the writer's text and suggest a sort of teacherly "marking" of a paper, putting us in a role of authority we don't want.

Advantages	*Disadvantages*
Interlaced comments show writers exactly the sections you're referring to.	If you place comments at the end, you'll have to quote the sections you're referring to, but that should be easy with some cut and paste, but once again you're appropriating the text, cutting it apart.

A more ideal situation would be a synchronous conference in which the paper could be in one window and the "conference" in another. You could have the paper sent to you in advance and you could paste it into a word-processing document, which could be running while you have a synchronous conference through Chat or at a MOO location. Then both you and the writer could cut and paste sections of the paper into the MOO to discuss. An even more ideal situation would be teleconferencing. But it is expensive and not available to very many writers—at least not yet. Both parties have to have compatible software to make it work, and we find that the more variables there are, the more things can go wrong. If the writer is in the local area, there's always the telephone, a very good way to personalize the conference.

RESPONSES TO E-TUTORING

The writers we interviewed were very positive about the tutoring exchange they had with us. They felt that their writing improved, and they enjoyed having to push their arguments more than they were used to doing.

A group of high school students we E-tutored also responded very positively to writing centers. Of a class of fourteen, six students contacted their high school teacher after graduation and told her that one of the first things they did when they got to college was to find the writing center and find out how to use it. These were students in an AP class, and their teacher was concerned that if they earned a 4 or a 5 on the AP test, they would place out of the first-year writing program, but they contacted the writing center and knew just where and how to get help with their writing.

E-TUTORING FRUSTRATIONS

One of the most frustrating things for tutors can be the thundering silence that follows an e-response to a paper. After the f2f session, the writer is likely to let us know that we were helpful. But what if you spend a significant amount of time thinking up and writing good questions for a writer and then hear nothing? Was the writer helped? We have no idea. All of us asked for feedback from the high school writers last spring, but heard nothing. (This year we changed that, and many of us saw second and even third drafts.) Our tutors were disappointed at how unsatisfying these one-way conferences felt compared to f2f, so do whatever you need to do to make the sessions interactive.

We think it would be frustrating, too, to get a draft from a writer who has a lot of problems with correctness. We feel that those writers would be helped best in person.

DON'T BLEED ON THE CUTTING EDGE

What we've described are just the very basics for on-line tutoring; however, we firmly believe that the sound practices that we described for f2f tutoring certainly apply. Nevertheless, some researchers feel that on-line tutoring makes some fundamental changes in how we perceive our work with writers (e.g., Coogan). The lack of visual clues and the need to make expectations and "rules" clear—and that this clarity must come through written text—are fascinating elements of on-line tutoring. The relationship that you create with writers is much more grounded in written text, whether that's the writer's paper-in-progress or the "conversation" you are having via synchronous or asynchronous means. We certainly can't declare that phenomenon good or bad; it simply *is*. And as institutions of learning increasingly turn to technology to deliver instruction, the on-line writing center will become much more the norm, if not the model for how to blend technology and pedagogy. If you're already an online tutor, we salute you. If you or your writing center are thinking of taking that "leap," we urge both caution and enthusiasm. We believe the ultimate goal is the development of the writer; we're hopeful that technology can help us to achieve that end.

13

WRITING CENTER ETHICS

Throughout this book we've offered practical advice, discussed some common challenges, and offered you a chance to learn about various aspects of writing center tutoring. While this information comes from our own experiences as writers, tutors, and writing center directors, it also comes from our ethics of tutoring.

We don't use the word *ethics* lightly. Ethics are usually associated with values and morals, a sense of right and wrong, a framework for behavior. In tutoring writing, ethics are synonymous with responsible conduct. For instance, as a tutor you're responsible to yourself, to the writers with whom you work, to your tutor colleagues, to your writing center director or equivalent, to your writing center itself, to your school, and even to the writing center field. Your conduct in any single session can have an impact on these various interested parties. For instance, showing up late to your tutoring shift can affect your own standing in the eyes of your director and of the writer signed up to meet with you, your colleagues' opinion of you, and your writing center's reputation. As a tutor, your responsible conduct has a ripple effect, demonstrating to all parties with a stake in the matter that the work you do is meaningful.

Your responsible conduct also has larger meaning in some of the fundamental ways we've talked about tutoring in this book, particularly in the contrast between tutors and editors. When we remind you that writers should "own" their texts or that tutors shouldn't simply "clean up" writers' texts and then hand them back as if we were a dry cleaner, we show certain values and responsibilities that imbue writing center work. Your work as a tutor will require an ethical code, a conscious system of behavior that is reasoned, thoughtful, and responsible. And this code includes not only "local" responsibilities (for instance, treating all writers and colleagues with respect, fulfilling your job's duties, not using the writing center as a dating service!), but responsibilities that you now bear as a member of the writing center field. After all, we want our work to be taken seriously by those outside of our field. Responsible conduct—and continual discussion and examination of those responsibilities—is essential to this goal.

As we've pointed out, however, tutoring is a complex matter. Certain situations will arise in your tutoring that challenge your beliefs about responsible conduct. In the next chapter, we'll focus on a wide variety of these challenges and give you some practical advice for "troubleshooting." In this chapter, we want to provide an overview of how you might understand and apply your ethics of tutoring and focus on a few particularly challenging scenarios. We also want to refer you to Michael Pemberton's frequent "Writing Center Ethics" columns in the *Writing Lab Newsletter*. Michael thoroughly discusses a variety of ethical situations and provides solid guidance that you'll find quite helpful in your development as a tutor.

WRITING CENTER MISSION STATEMENTS

A tutor's idea of responsible conduct should flow naturally from a larger idea of the writing center's ethics. If you are unsure of the ethical code of your writing center, one of the best places to discover that is in your center's mission statement. Below are excerpts from the University of Texas at Austin Undergraduate Writing Center's Mission Statement. Notice how tutor and writer responsibilities are defined and how the work of the center is discussed with expressed understanding of what learning and teaching writing means:

> *Our goal is to help undergraduate students grow and mature as writers by providing help with difficulties, situational or otherwise, they may have in academic writing. Primarily, we do this in individual tutorials, called consultations, in which a student works one-on-one with a Graduate or Undergraduate Writing Consultant.*
>
> *We envision our role as that of professional consultants. In many activities that require complex skills and demand practice people take lessons from experts or hire professional consultants. For example, people take golf lessons or cooking classes to become better golfers or more versatile cooks, and businesses hire consultants to improve their performance. The advice that experts provide for these purposes is not punitive, not judgmental, and not remedial, because it is sought after and valued. The consultant views her client as a competent adult who is not an expert in her own field. In our work with students, we use the terms "problems," "difficulties," and "help" advisedly. All writers can have problems, but student writers are often prob-*

lematized in ways that other writers with problems are not. For example, a professor revising an article for publication may need to know that her ideas are clear to a reader. She has a problem that she can solve without defining herself as a "problem writer" by asking a colleague to read her draft and make comments. A writing center should answer students' needs for interested, helpful, but nonjudgmental readers like the professor's colleague. A few of the difficulties student writers encounter, such as inadequate preparation for the intellectual and stylistic demands of college writing, may be unique to writers still in college. But undergraduates are not the only writers to encounter difficulties. More experienced, confident writers may experience difficulties with writing, for example, when they try to write about complex and unfamiliar material, when they face writing tasks that are new to them, when the material or social conditions in which they must work are detrimental to their writing process, or when they are distracted by other concerns. Student writers face many of the same problems, and they deserve our attention and respect when they attempt to address them.

The help we provide is intended to foster independence. We do not, therefore, edit or proofread student papers. Instead, we teach students how to edit and proofread their own work more accurately and efficiently. Advice given in consultations is professional but nondirective. The invention of ideas and supporting statements remains the writer's responsibility. The consultation belongs to the student. This is why students have access to the records we keep of their work with us and why we do not notify teachers of their students' visits if students ask us not to.

If your center does not have a mission statement, we recommend that you speak with your director about taking on the task of drafting one. Not only will the mission statement give the tutors a clear sense of philosophy, goals, and responsibilities, but you can then share that mission with writers who come to you, heading off miscommunication about what the center does and does not do.

Another important source for the ethics of your center is to examine your school or college's mission statement. For example, the Massachusetts College of Pharmacy and Health Sciences Mission Statement states several "core values," including "innovative teaching which fosters student-centered learning." The statement notes that "the College reaches these goals by providing a state-of-the-art learning environment which facilitates critical thinking and problem-solving skills." To fulfill this mission, "active learning will be fostered by innovative and creative teaching methods." In many ways, the values embodied by these statements speak of writing as a tool of learning, the value of one-to-one instruction and student support, and a commitment to student-centered learning. It's not unreasonable, then, to extend from these ideas notions of attention to the writers' processes rather than their products, and student ownership of their texts (and their learn-ing). Our point here is that the line from the ethics of tutoring to the ethics of the entire institution should, ideally, be a straight one. If you've never read your school or college's mission statement, seek it out. After all, it provides a description for responsible conduct that you are expected to abide by.

TUTOR AND WRITER RESPONSIBILITIES

In our chapter on how your expectations for tutoring writing might have been formed, we showed how these expectations strongly affect what you hold your responsibilities to be, as well as those of the writers with whom you'll work. These notions are shaped by your ethics of tutoring, by your sense of responsible conduct. As we pointed out, all too often your expecta-tions can be influenced by forces you're not entirely aware of: your previous experiences (both good and bad), your culture, your prejudices.

An important part of being an ethical tutor is to treat writers (and their texts) with respect, admiration, and sensitivity. We can tell you now that you'll work with writers who will challenge these ideas, ones who won't treat you with the same qualities. But that leads to the question of just what are the responsibilities of writers. Here's how some of the tutor trainees at Marquette addressed this issue:

From Jessica:

> Writers should be attentive, open to new ideas, be willing to change and establish new habits. They must be sincere in their intentions. Writers as well as tutors must be good listeners.

From Adele:

> The writer has the responsibilities of being a critical thinker and an hon-est person. If either tutor or writer does not understand something, then they [should] ask. Honesty and clarity are what make the whole equa-tion work. The writer also must be open-minded, as well as the tutor, and willing to consider different approaches to writing.

From Kristina:

> The writer is responsible for making the paper what he or she wants to make it. He or she accomplishes this by engaging in conversation with the tutor about the paper, answering the questions the tutor asks, criti-

cally thinking about the paper as the discussion moves along, and writing things down along the way.

From Shantel:

> The major responsibility of the "tutee" is to want the help offered, be willing to accept what the tutor has to say, be able to take constructive criticism, and be open to new suggestions. Also, having a paper written and ready to be evaluated is kind of important. Lastly, the thing a student should be responsible for is treating the tutor with respect.

From Angela:

> The students should not totally rely on the tutors to get the wheels churning in their minds. Students should come with their best draft, so that progress can be made. Also, they should be able to answer questions [such as] what they like about the paper, what they don't like, etc. This way, even if they don't know exactly what they want to do with the paper, they know what should stay, or what should change.

From Jason:

> The writer must be an active part in the tutoring process. The writer cannot expect to be a "mental sponge" and absorb all the information from the tutor. Instead, the tutor and the writer must work as a team to achieve the desired results (the improvement of the writer).

From Sara:

> Writers have the responsibility of communication. After all, that should be the goal of whatever they are working on—to communicate to a given audience. As we listen, provide feedback, and ask questions, they need to work on trying to improve the way they communicate through their papers. Part of this is being willing to talk to us about their desires for their papers—what they want to say, what is working, what is not working.

From Aesha:

> The writer is responsible to utilize the skills already present in him/herself. He/she must be willing to try something different, move out of the comfort zone. He/she must recognize the fact that the tutor is someone

who can help him/her do what he/she already knows how to do and not do it for them.

We're sure that you had similar responsibilities in mind when you considered the question of writer responsibilities. Each of the trainees describes a fairly active role for the writer, one that reciprocates the hard work that the tutor is demonstrating and one that is in the writer's best interests. However, think in broader terms where these expectations might have come from. Are they products of value systems, of culture? How are they confounded when a writer has a very different sense of personal distance or politeness or authority, as many writers from countries outside of the United States (or from a different culture than yours) will have? And how "empowered" are some writers to own their texts in the face of poorly conceived assignments or dull course work? Do many writers have a voice outside of the writing center to register meaningful protest or do something about aspects of their schooling that they are unhappy with?

Even in the writing center, writers don't necessarily have the same rights and obligations as tutors. We think Andy zeroed in on this dilemma in his response to the question of writers' responsibilities:

> I realize more and more students are aware of the way the writing center works, so their expectations are being met more and more often. However, students are not part of this dialogue about what their responsibilities are, what tutors expect of them, so how can they be prepared to meet expectations?

Andy nicely makes our point here. Your sense of writing center ethics will determine just what you believe your and the writers' responsibilities are to be. However, it's important that you give writers a voice in determining how a session is run. Certainly, we all cringe at those requests for "proofreading" or "grammar checking," but we caution you to look beyond those convenient labels (or at least investigate why the writers are issuing these sorts of requests).

The work of tutoring, in its collaborative approach to learning, in its student-centered values, and its emphasis on finding meaning and fostering communication, can be quite unlike anything else that happens at your school or college. Thus, the way you treat writers and the opportunities you offer them are important to think about. An essential part of being an ethical tutor is to be constantly examining your belief systems. Certain students will challenge those beliefs with their behavior, but rather than dismiss the behavior as wrong, think about why you believe as you do and how your actions demonstrate those beliefs. We believe that ethical tutors are reflective, questioning, and constantly learning (an indication of *our* ethics as writing center directors and textbook authors).

CHALLENGES TO THE ETHICAL TUTOR

In the next chapter, we run through a variety of scenarios that will challenge you as a tutor, and we provide some practical advice for dealing with those situations. In this chapter, we want to focus in on two particular types of situations, ones that we hope you don't have to experience, but if you do, we want you to be prepared.

Scenario #1—The writer has plagiarized.

There are many variations on this scenario. Most commonly, writers will unintentionally plagiarize, whether that means not citing someone else's words or ideas or not paraphrasing well and instead presenting nearly word-for-word what someone else wrote. For these writers, it's important that you probe their knowledge of plagiarism. Most often, you'll find that they just haven't learned the correct method for citing sources or that they come from a culture with a very different sense of intellectual property. A brief tour of the handbook or some exercise in accurate paraphrasing will fix matters.

Hopefully less often, you'll encounter a writer who has deliberately plagiarized. The writer might admit this act to you (as has happened to us, pulling us in as "coconspirators" in the activity) or the writer will deny something you know to be true (because you know the original essay or you saw another writer earlier in the day with the identical paper). As an ethical tutor, what do you do? What's your responsibility for enforcing what is in almost all places a serious violation, one that could result in failure, suspension, or dismissal?

Most important is to know your writing center's and director's policy in such matters. Most writing center directors will take on the responsibility of deciding whether or not to contact the writer's class instructor. But this is an important topic to bring up in your staff meetings or in a training class; better to know policy before the problem occurs.

At some schools and colleges, all students are held to an honor code, and that often includes the responsibility for reporting on violations, as well as upholding the code yourself. If you're using this type of system, the procedures should be clear cut, but again this is an important topic to bring up in class or meetings before you're called upon to take action.

Scenario #2—The writer's point of view is one you find offensive.

There's nothing to challenge our sense of writer empowerment and owner-ship like one whose views we find utterly offensive. Certainly there will be writers who take stands with which we disagree, but in this scenario we're talking about views you find reprehensible or personally troubling. Is it your ethical responsibility to set this writer straight? Rather than say, "Well, any argument is strengthened by acknowledging the views of the opposing side. So what are some of the counterarguments that you've considered?" does your mind race with personal insults (which you suppress), but then a list of logical points in opposition to the writer's viewpoint? In the following ex-cerpt from her paper, Stephanie Wankum encountered just this dilemma:

> During my fifth tutoring session, I had a head-on collision with a paper that struck me in a personal manner. The student's assignment was to present a common and widely accepted view about a particular issue and then present "bad news" that would cause the audience to question the common view. The tutee's paper was about chemotherapy and the com-mon view was supposed to be that chemotherapy is considered a great treatment. I thought "chemotherapy is *not* considered good." Then I thought "wait—maybe people do think it's good." How could I *not* know?
>
> Chemotherapy is a personal issue for me. My mother was on che-motherapy while I was growing up. When the student started to reveal all the bad things about chemotherapy, I found that I wasn't able to con-centrate. I was back at the question about the common view. Was the common view he presented valid and was I unable to see it because I take for granted that everyone knows that chemotherapy is a horrible treatment? Perhaps I know this only because I have dealt with it person-ally. I had to confront this issue quickly and began searching for a way to do it. I mentally started to reflect on class discussions and preparation that dealt directly with the issue of personal disagreement. I realized that I may be opposed to the student's thesis statement because I have personal knowledge about the subject, but more importantly, because it makes me emotional. I also knew that I should be able to step back and consider the paper in an objective manner.
>
> When I began to consider the paper objectively, I realized that my initial reaction was not as personal as I originally thought. I simply con-sidered what my peers might think about chemotherapy. Most of them did not grow up directly involved with the treatment and surely would not claim that the common view of chemotherapy was that it was a good treatment.

The student had finished reading his paper and was silently waiting for me to say something. I was still mentally playing tennis with the idea of common view when I realized that I had to go on with the session. I procrastinated by asking him to outline his thesis statement. I started asking more questions and eventually my mental limbo began to work itself out. The nondirective tutoring style of questioning helped me to do this.

Tutor training taught my class that nondirective tutoring was the preferred method of tutoring because it allowed students to figure things out for themselves. I would not have guessed that it would help me figure things out as well. The more I questioned the student the more I was aware that this assumption of the common view was incorrect. Question-oriented tutoring eased the confusion of my personal dilemma. This tutoring style shaped the session and began to give it direction. The student finally came to a point at which he admitted that he never thought that chemotherapy was a great treatment. When he left he said that he didn't plan to change the paper but was going to remodel how he presented the common view. As I wished him good luck, I felt relief and consciously realized that I had made a connection between two concepts discussed in training.

When I began tutoring, I was aware of directive and nondirective tutoring styles, how to be professional in the face of opposition, and even where the tissues are located. I did not know then that circumstance would weave some of these concepts together. In this particular circumstance I realized that nondirective tutoring can help the tutor as much as the student. I needed to muddle through the process of severing personal and professional views. Class discussion created an awareness of the need for such severing. The discussions also taught my class how to help the student wade through issues of clarity by utilizing nondirective methods and forms of questioning. I have discovered that the tutoring techniques that help students understand what to do in a session are the same ones that help the tutor understand what direction to take.

As Stephanie shows, she was committed to an ethical view of tutoring. She was challenged by the desire to counter the writer's expressed point of view, but ultimately she relied upon what she felt to be responsible conduct—with this or any other writer.[1]

---

[1]For another example of how to work with a writer who has objectionable views, see Jay D. Sloan's article on the National Writing Center Association's website: http://departments.colgate.edu/diw/NWCAStories.html

The ethics of tutoring writing are brought to bear in every session you observe or participate in. The behaviors you see or enact all have reason, all have a certain motivation. Our point is that what you do as a tutor should flow from your idea of responsible conduct and that conduct should be carefully thought out and consciously examined. You will be challenged by writers who don't—at least initially—share your sense of responsibilities or standards of ethical behavior. But it is in that challenge that you can strengthen your beliefs, as Stephanie did, and help the writer to more fully explore her point of view.

14

TROUBLESHOOTING

We've tried our best to help you develop techniques to take you through sessions in which things go smoothly. But what about those times when they don't? The more you observe, the more you will see that not all sessions are ideal. Over the years, our staffs have encountered many troublesome situations, and we find that it helps to be prepared. The staff of tutors you will be working with will have encountered these situations, too, and will have come up with approaches of their own, so you don't have to figure all these situations out yourself; do ask the experienced tutors for their advice.

Here are some scenarios that we've run into, and we make suggestions for ways to cope. These are *only* suggestions, though. In some cases they will work, and in others they could be awful. Use your best judgment in these difficult situations, and ask for advice.

YOU SUSPECT THE WRITER MIGHT HAVE A LEARNING DISABILITY (LD)

Perhaps a writer is hesitant to read a draft to you. He asks you to read it, and when you do, you find it is full of errors, particularly reversed letters, too many for a student at his educational level. Or perhaps you have him read aloud, and his reading is labored and full of errors that might not be on the page. You begin to wonder if he has a learning disability.

Learning disorders manifest themselves in many forms and have a wide range of severity. So it's hard to make generalizations about a single way to proceed. Nevertheless, the basic tutoring principles of careful listening and observing and being sensitive to the writer's specific needs apply with LD writers, just as they do with all. Still, it's good to keep a few things in mind before you start, particularly for newly diagnosed LD writers, who will be experiencing the most difficulty with coping and will need the most help:

To ask or not to ask: We think it's better for LD writers to self-identify. Some of them will send a letter to the writing center, via the school's LD specialist. Some will just volunteer that they are LD. But some will prefer just to work on their writing in their own terms. If you wonder if it's appropriate to ask, check with your director first to see what your writing center's policy is.

Confidentiality: Suppose the writer has identified herself as having a learning disability. She has a right to her privacy on this matter, and might prefer not to have friends and casual acquaintances know all about her, so don't discuss this writer's problems with friends or colleagues. It may be appropriate to discuss strategies for working with LD writers in staff meetings, but keep your discussion private and professional.

Dealing with difference: The written page might not look the same to the LD writer as it does for you. He might not be able to see spelling errors at all (and a spell checker does a lot, but leaves a lot undone, too, as we all know). He might not be able to spot grammatical errors, either, and will need help finding them. Also, LD writers are generally of average or above-average intelligence; poor spelling is certainly not an indication of low intelligence!

Talk about strategies: You'll discover that some LD writers evolve very ingenious ways of getting around their disability and are themselves your best resource in the tutorial. The writer has had a long time to adjust to his disability and probably knows very well what kinds of help he needs. Listen to him and take lots of cues from him. Work to help him refine his strategic repertoire by asking about his methods for success in a variety of tasks, even nonwritten ones. You will need to be flexible, patient, and creative in your sessions.

Be positive: Your tone of friendly acceptance will help writers to feel more comfortable with a task they probably find formidable.

Finding a topic and getting started: Sometimes the LD writer will need your help brainstorming. Many LD writers know a great deal about the subjects they must write about, but come to sessions thinking they have no ideas to work with. For many LD writers, the typical brainstorming techniques we use—freewriting, for example—might not lead to useful writing ideas. Instead, your questions will help them develop their ideas. Some will need you to write down key terms or take notes as you ask them questions about the subject matter. Some may need you to help them organize their ideas into an outline. If you suggest a technique and the writer resists it, trust her.

Working with error: The LD writer might not be able to see an error until it is pointed out. Expect her to be well-acquainted with the spell-checker on her computer. But don't necessarily expect her to be able to see the misspelled word the way you do. Help her to find it, and then help her to correct it. She'll probably have a very good memory, and hearing the word spelled correctly might be all she needs. If you read a sentence aloud, the LD writer is likely to be able to catch and correct it. You can help the writer make a list of words to have the computer search for, if she is able to see and correct her errors once they are pointed out.

Leave extra time: You might need to schedule an extra-long session or multiple sessions with the LD writer.

Finding space: Some LD writers need a quiet, uncluttered space. Some writers will have attention-deficit disorder and will find a noisy room a huge distraction. See if you can find a quiet space to work.

Seek out expertise: Most schools will have a learning-disabled student specialist or an office of disabled students, which has access to this expertise. Talk with your director about bringing in an LD specialist to better inform the writing center staff.

THE PAPER IS ALL MARKED UP

An instructor has scribbled all over the draft, corrected errors, and written so many comments in the margin that it's hard to see the writer's text. The writer needs to revise. In many cases, the writer will want to do only what he has been commanded in red ink to do, and it makes the session difficult, since you and the writer, if allowed to use his own judgment, might come to different revision strategies, not the ones suggested by the teacher. The decision is whether to give the instructor exactly what she wants or to go for a different revision strategy. It might help to ask the writer if he has the document on disk. You could run off a clean copy and see what the two of you come up with and then compare notes with what the teacher has suggested. If that isn't practical, it might be good to ignore, at first, what the instructor has said, and make the revisions the writer thinks are important. Try to keep in mind that whatever chaos the situation creates for you, the instructor meant well, and may well have done this marking out of exasperation. Try, at all costs, to keep your feelings or biases toward minimal marking out of a session such as this.

THE GRADE ON A WRITER'S PAPER SEEMS UNFAIR

Case A—The grade seems unfairly low to you.

First, remember that it's not our function to whip the teaching staff into shape. It's our job to help the writer deal with his writing contexts, including the instructor. Any remarks we might pass about a grade could very well get exaggerated and repeated to that person. Second, remember that we don't know about all the verbal contracts the teacher and the writer have. A paper that looks fine to us might be off the topic, or the writer might have forgotten or ignored some verbal instruction the teacher set up in class, instructions that might not appear in print. It's best not to betray to the writer any reaction you might have about the fairness of the grade. If she asks your opinion point blank, tell her you are not in a position to make such a judgment. If the situation disturbs you, bring it up at a staff meeting (without mentioning the name of the instructor) or talk to your director. Every center will have its own way of dealing with such situations.

Case B—The grade seems unfairly low to the writer.

If you've ever been in this kind of situation, you know what kind of stress the writer is bringing to this conference, so it will be hard to find the right balance between making him feel all right about himself and taking his side. Don't let yourself be called in as an expert on what grade a paper deserves. You can read the paper over and try to help the writer understand the instructor's comments, if this seems appropriate, but avoid taking sides. If, after you've gone over the comments, the writer is convinced that the grade is truly unfair, he can appeal the grade, and deserves to know what the process is. The question is whether you should suggest such a course of action. The first and best suggestion is to have the writer discuss the grade with the instructor. If the writer were to initiate a grade appeal, this would be his first step, anyway, in most schools, and nothing would be done until this was initiated. Often the instructor is able to explain the grade in a way that satisfies the writer. If the writer has spoken to the instructor and hasn't been given any help in understanding the grade, he can pursue the grade appeal process. Ask your director about this. But regardless of how you feel about the grade's fairness, this is one of those times when you'll need to keep your opinions to yourself. We rely a great deal on the good will and open communication and cooperation we have established with the teaching staff. They trust us, and this is the reason we see so many of their writers. Criticizing them to their writers in any way will erode that trust pretty quickly.

THE WRITER DEMANDS A LETTER GRADE

Tell the writer that to guess at a grade is absolutely against your policy, and that you will get into trouble if you do it. Refer her to the director if she insists.

THE WRITER COMES IN AND ASKS YOU TO PROOFREAD

There's no need to tip your hand too early. Don't say, "We don't proofread," or the writer may just leave. Tell the writer that you'll begin the session by listening to the paper and looking at larger issues first. Then, if there's no time to get to proofreading after you've discussed higher-order concerns, point out one or two things you noticed (if you noticed anything at all) for the writer to work on and urge her to come back to look at surface errors. And remember, you can't *hear* certain errors; you'll have to *see* them, so don't be too quick to reassure the writer that the paper is free of errors. But it makes no sense to correct the errors in a paper that needs revision, and some writers will not change or move or strike out a section, no matter how badly it fits into a paper, once it's been corrected for errors.

THE PAPER IS DUE SOON!

It makes a huge difference whether the paper is due in a day or an hour. If the writer has a day to work on it, proceed as usual, looking at higher-order concerns. But urge the writer to make an appointment for earlier in the writing process. If the paper is due in an hour, then don't ask the writer to read aloud; help her look for errors, but don't hesitate to point out structural elements that need revision. There might be time for her to make some significant revisions while correcting errors. Be tactful as you urge these writers to come earlier. Surely some of them will have tried to, but will not have been able to get an earlier appointment.

THE WRITER IS CRYING

Get to know where to find a box of tissues. Leaving for a minute to get a few will give the writer a chance to regain his composure, and give you a chance to work out a strategy. When you get back with the tissues (bring plenty; this may be a long session), ask the writer if he would like to be alone for a minute. If not, it wouldn't hurt to try some Rogerian techniques, repeating to the writer or paraphrasing what he has said to you: he says, "I'm so stressed." You say, "You seem pretty upset." This helps the writer get things out. Remember, though, that we are not the counseling center, and if the writer's upset seems serious, or if he is crying for what doesn't seem to you to be anything serious, or if he comes in and cries at more than one session, ask if he has heard of the counseling center or student support service on your campus. Sometimes we are the first to see a student's true stress or depression, because writing on sensitive topics or getting a bad grade can trigger these outward signs of upset. Sometimes the cause is time management and grade pressure, and then your student retention counselor will be able to help. The important thing is to let the writer have space and time to regain composure and to suggest some people he can contact. Look up the numbers, if he seems interested in getting help, or call and hand the phone over to him. It wouldn't hurt to follow up on this writer, either, perhaps with a call the next day to make sure he's all right.

THE WRITER WON'T REVISE

A few years ago we had a writer who would come in for regular appointments, as many a week as we would give him, work with the same tutor, but expect to make all his revisions during the session. He would come in with his paper unchanged for the next session. Now this can happen to the most conscientious of writers: They run out of time before their next appointment, but this writer developed a pattern of never revising outside of the appointment. The tutor felt that she was doing too much and that he had to take responsibility for his work. Eventually she told him that he would have to make revisions if he wanted to have another appointment. It turned out that he lacked the confidence to make the changes himself, but his confidence grew as he observed the revision process taking place during the sessions. It just took him a while to get the hang of revising papers.

THE WRITER WON'T LISTEN

You recognize that a paper is deeply flawed and you've tried to get the writer to see what you see by asking questions about it. The writer insists that she likes everything in the paper, sometimes the very things that make the paper weak. Your well-intentioned questions don't work. Finally you might try saying, "Such and such just doesn't work for me." The writer still likes the entire thing. One of our staff members once said, "You can lead a horse to water, but you can't make him freewrite." After suggesting that the writer show the draft to the instructor, give up gracefully. Not everyone is meant to be helped. But be comforted: Maybe after the writer leaves, she will rethink her decisions or see her instructor.

THE WRITER IS DEPENDENT

If we have plenty of open time in our schedule, we let writers schedule multiple appointments in a week. Last year we had an absolutely delightful writer from India. She had a standing appointment to improve her writing (though she was a very good writer), but before papers were due, she would schedule a number of appointments with various tutors. Yet we never considered her dependent. Why? Because between sessions she revised and improved her papers. She took our questions to heart and did excellent revisions, then wanted more feedback, often from another reader. Late in the semester she mentioned that the tutors in the writing center were her only friends. We asked her if she knew about the international student associations, and to our surprise, she said she had never heard of them. The turnaround was immediate and dramatic. She called that day, found that there was going to be a celebration of Diwali, the Indian festival of lights, and she signed on and became involved. She still came in for tutoring, but less often, and she invited us to the celebrations and came in one day to paint the tutors' hands with henna. So coming to get help often doesn't necessarily imply dependence. She had just found a friendly place where she got good work done.

But we've had writers who were completely dependent, such as the example above of the writer who wouldn't revise. One of our tutors became frustrated with him at one point and asked if he could be switched to another tutor. We encourage tutors to ask for this if they need to.

THE WRITER IS TUTOR SURFING

You have an appointment with a writer. You notice as you glance over the schedule that she is also seeing two other tutors that day and two the next. She is tutor surfing. Now, there are good reasons to do this. She may be looking for someone who has the right chemistry to work with her. We've seen this with writers who had worked regularly with a tutor who graduated. And once we had a very canny writer who liked to brainstorm with one tutor, show a first draft to another, polish a draft with a third, and look for errors with a fourth. He was a true writing center connoisseur. We all looked forward to working with him and enjoyed his expertise in writing center nuances. But there are bad and counterproductive reasons for tutor surfing. Sometimes writers are very scared of a paper assignment and want to get as many appointments as they can. Occasionally they are hoping that they'll find a tutor who actually will proofread for them, so they come in again and again and ask for the same thing. These writers will make much better progress with fewer appointments but with the same tutor, and usually all we have to do is point this out to them, and then they make a choice. And it's an informed choice, since by then they know us all.

THE WRITER IS NOT COOPERATING

Sometimes a writer will schedule an appointment and sit sullenly, say "I don't know" when you ask questions, or give monosyllabic and unenthusiastic replies. One of our writers, when asked to read her paper aloud, showed her rebellion by stuffing her mouth full of peanuts and mumbling as she chewed them. The members of our staff began to refer to these uncooperative types as "peanut people." Sometimes it's possible to find out what's bothering them and correct it.

Were they forced to come? Ask, "What made you decide to come here?" They'll tell you if they were required to attend. Some classes have a regular policy of making students use the writing center. Some instructors give extensions to writers who will seek tutoring. Sometimes these restrictions make the writers resentful, and they don't put much into the sessions. We try to let instructors know in our public relations material that requiring writing center sessions can backfire, and our policy is that when writers don't do their part, we tell them, quite courteously, that they can go. Sometimes just letting them off the hook makes them thaw out and want to be part of the session.

Did we fail to meet their expectations? Sometimes writers hear that we will proofread. We try hard to let them know what we do. We visit classes and spread the word, but sometimes writers get bad information anyway. By the time the writer is glaring and sullen, it may be too late, but if it's the writer's first session, it helps to sketch out what will happen, so she can say, "Whoa! I'm leaving. I wanted proofreading." Often, though, writers are convinced to stay.

Sometimes there are no reasons we can discern for what might seem like sullen, uncooperative behavior. If you ask a question and there's no answer, there's a good chance the writer is just mulling over the possibilities. Try not to jump to conclusions about a quiet writer. Some writers are more passive than others, and if you will jump in and answer your own questions, they will quickly catch on and wait you out. Turn the tables by waiting them out. If there is a long pause, you might ask them to jot down a few ideas while you take a short break. Sometimes writing can break a mental logjam.

THE WRITER FRIGHTENS YOU

We don't think it's a good idea to work with someone who scares you. Once a tutor of ours got a writer angry by insisting that he read his paper aloud. She felt that because it was our policy, that she was required to do it. It really made this student uncomfortable and very threatened, because he was struggling as a writer and he was not a fluent reader. When he became angry, he really frightened the tutor, because the writer was quite large and really agitated. This would have been a good time to let go of our policy and do what the writer needed, but the tutor felt strongly that she was doing the right thing. Don't hesitate to ask someone else to take an angry or upsetting writer. This is what the tutor did. The writer began to work with a different tutor and came in for help for several years as he finished his degree. In the Marquette Writing Center, we have a very broadly worded conduct statement posted that says:

> *The Norman H. Ott Memorial Writing Center expects those who use our services to respect the rights of others. Responsible conduct is expected and required. Individuals who engage in unacceptable behavior such as physical and/or verbal abuse may lose their writing center privileges and/or be subject to university disciplinary action.*

If a writer is verbally or in some other way abusive, you have a right to ask him or her to leave, as long as you have posted some kind of notice. If there is no conduct statement in your center, we strongly suggest that you get one (see also Eric Hobson's article "An Ounce of Prevention: Ensuring Safety in the Writing Center" in *The Writing Lab Newsletter,* June 1997).

THE WRITER HAS CHOSEN A REALLY BAD TOPIC

Case 1—The topic is clichéd.

Sometimes we'll hear what a writer is working on and we'll groan, thinking that the topic is really bad, only to discover that she's worked wonders with it. Recently a writer came in and announced that her paper was about bees. The topic was to find something that most people view negatively and share some surprising good news about it. Two of the three sample essays from the textbook were about spiders, so when Kristin announced that she was writing about bees, Paula felt apprehensive. She had formed an ideal text, or rather formed a text, and it wasn't ideal at all. Paula was afraid that the writer's essay would be a close imitation of those samples in the book. But then the writer told Paula that her good news was that bee stings were being used as alternative medicine for such serious problems as arthritis and MS. When she told Paula that she'd gotten her information from her mother, who had MS, the topic really seemed interesting, and Paula could see that her topic, far from being weak, was very interesting. Paula learned a lot as the writer read her drafts aloud.

But some topics truly are clichéd, and it's very difficult to say new things about them. Most teachers will rattle off a list of topics they never want to see again, because the opposing sides have been discussed to death. We need to remember, though, that one person's cliché is another person's news flash. So it's important to be tactful when we help writers think more critically about topics that are new and vibrant to them. One way to get them to dig more deeply is to invite them to use what Peter Elbow and Pat Belanoff call the Loop Process. You begin by having the writer jot down all his first thoughts and preconceptions on a topic, and then urge him to go deeper, to find the corner of the topic that's meaningful for him. Ask him to think about the audience: What does the audience already know? What do they need to know? Sometimes, however, a conference with a teacher might be the only way to get a writer to choose a better topic.

Case 2—The topic doesn't fit the assignment.

As much as we want to foster creativity and independent thinking, choosing a topic that doesn't meet the assignment is likely to get the writer a bad grade, regardless of how well he's written on it. He needs to be told that his assignment is off the topic, and you will be able to help him find another. This is very hard for a writer. He's invested a lot of energy in his topic, and he might not seem glad to be told that his topic is off, but depending on his goals for the course, he will thank you later. Urge him to ask his instructor if the topic is in doubt.

Case 3—The topic is off the wall.

One of our trainees observed a session in which the writer's topic was to describe a time when he had changed his mind. He chose to write about the experience of using a public bathroom in his residence hall. The details he included seemed inappropriate for the topic, and the trainee wondered how she'd get the writer to see this without being directive. But the tutor had had plenty of experience, and he knew what to do. He focused on the assignment and asked the writer how he had changed his mind. The writer agreed that he hadn't really written about a change of mind, so he changed his topic. It would be good to discuss this topic with your fellow tutors and your director to see how your center handles these kinds of situations.

THE WRITER IS EMOTIONALLY INVESTED IN THE PAPER AND CAN'T WRITE IT

You have several options. You can help the writer find a part of the assignment that isn't so close to home. Brainstorm with him about the topic in general, staying away from his personal story, but talking about the issues involved. As you brainstorm, you might find some topics that interest him in an intellectual way, that are distanced from an experience that might be painful for him. You can also help him talk through the difficulty so that he better understands his deep investment in the topic and so that he is able to write a version of the paper. You can also suggest a visit with the instructor, to talk things over.

THE WRITER'S PAPER IS FULL OF ERRORS

Persist in your policy of looking at the higher-order concerns first, but point out to the writer before the session is over that you saw a lot of errors, and show her a few. Urge her to come back with a revision, if possible, to work on them. If that is not possible, get her to ask a friend to help her spot them. Remember that some errors are a function of the writer's weak grasp of the subject matter. As she revises and rethinks her topic, sometimes those errors go away on their own and the writing flows more smoothly and correctly. If there is time do an error analysis with the writer, perhaps you can focus on one or two patterns of error.

THE WRITER CAN'T RECOGNIZE ERRORS

This writer needs help, and lots of it. Urge him to make a standing appointment, weekly, to get this problem under control. It's best to work with his own writing rather than doing exercises from a handbook, so have him bring in his work or write on the spot.

YOU FEEL THE WRITER STILL HAS FAR TO GO

The session has ended, but there is still much to do. Some tutors like to give the writer three things to work on. If the writer has time before the assignment is due, urge her to come back. If possible, help her set up an appointment, with you if at all possible. If only proofreading is left to finish and the deadline is near, suggest that writers seek out classmates for help. Urge international writers to ask their American friends to help them proofread. Don't let writers take advantage of you. When your time is up, tell the writer so, and don't feel guilty. Keeping a watch or clock on your desk will help both you and the writer remember to stay within time limits.

THE WRITER WON'T QUIT

A good way to avoid this situation is, about five minutes before the session ends, to begin to ask the writer what her plans are for revision. This communicates that the session is coming to an end, and helps the writer do some good work, consolidating her gains. If the writer persists, a tactful approach is for you to say, "Did the session help you?" If this doesn't work, stand up and say, "I enjoyed working with you. Another writer is waiting to see me," or whatever may be appropriate.

In a reflection paper, Angela Jesik discusses two less-than-perfect sessions that she encountered as she was just beginning her training process:

Tapping my fingers impatiently on the desk in Room 489, I grew anxious and nervous about observing my first session. I didn't know what to expect. I only assumed that I was about to witness the "tutor's magic," that specialized knowledge where they know the perfect questions to ask at precisely the right time to make the students discuss and improve their papers. As my mind drifted into scenarios of myself actually having that "magic," the student walked in, and it was time to observe the expert tutor at work.

First, Maggie, the student, explained the objective of the paper. She was to write an essay illustrating a point in her life when she changed her mind. She decided to write about how she grew up in Asia, hated America when she first moved back, and eventually accepted the American way of life. This essay seemed to be interesting, but I noticed Stewart, the tutor, grow tense with every sentence read. He did not behave in this manner because he was nervous like myself, but because each statement was insulting and ridiculed Americans. However, Maggie did not view her statements as offensively as did Stewart and I. She felt that these were her first impressions and refused to tone down her strong sentiments. After a few moments of composing himself, Stewart began to ask questions to help improve her paper. But, no matter how many questions he asked, and how forward he tried to be without being "directive," he could not make her understand that this language might insult the reader. It was in watching this deadlock between the tutor and the tutee that my whole world came crashing down upon me.

I wondered to myself, "What was going on?" "Why isn't she responding to his questions like the way we practiced in class?" And most importantly, "Where was his special tutor insight that would help this girl with the paper?" Although I had many questions, none of them were answered for me at that time. I left the session feeling distressed because I had witnessed the transformation of a "super tutor" into an average student with struggles just like me.

So, observing this did not give me an overabundant amount of confidence for my first tutoring session. If a person employed at the tutoring center had difficulties, how in the world was I going to help students with their papers? This thought resonated in my head as I introduced myself to my first tutee. To my dismay, she was an ESL student. Now, I have absolutely no prejudice against these students, but I knew that this session would be extra challenging, and honestly, I did not know if I was prepared. As I expected, this session went nothing like the "ideal ones" we had read or practiced. The student, Tracy, didn't even have a rough draft of her paper. She simply came in and said she had to write a four-page paper on the poem "Laguna Blues," and wanted me to explain it to her. Desperately scanning my memory for tips from class, the only thing I remembered was *"Don't be directive."* So I told her I would assist her in interpreting the material herself.

As the session progressed, I again tried to think of all the practice tutorials we had in class and the sessions I had observed, searching for the exact questions to help Tracy understand the material. But even though I tried and tried and tried, I couldn't recall any examples from class that would help me in this situation. I realized I was on my own, and that it was not the textbook scenarios we practiced in class, but my own interpretation of the material that was going to lead me to the next question. So, hands clenched, gnawing on my pen cap, I continued to discuss the poem with her.

Although it was perturbing and tedious, the session actually ended on a positive note. And, as I sighed with relief, Tracy told me I had helped her tremendously. It was at that moment I began to reflect upon my experience at the writing center. I realized that, from the beginning of class to the present, my whole opinion had changed. I used to believe that the writing center tutors knew everything, and that every session would be ideal. But, through my observations and experiences, I now realize there is no "magic formula" for being a tutor. Every session is unique, and every student will have a different attitude regarding the session. The only way to truly be a successful tutor is through a whole-hearted attempt to understand the assignment and the student. It is this individualized assessment, and not writing book guidelines, that will provide the foundation for improvement.

As I continue to observe and tutor, I do so with a fresh consciousness. I am no longer confined by the ideal classroom simulations. I have too much experience to believe that, once we write our names down in the appointment book, we are given supernatural tutor powers. I realize these expert tutors are experts only because they have experienced similar tutoring situations. Their expectations have also been built up by hearing about perfect sessions, only to have them crash down in real life. But what makes them different from novices is they understand that the key to effective tutoring is being adaptable and flexible. And, most importantly, they know the only "secret formula" to tutoring is not to expect anything that is ideal or easy.

Angela is right: There may be no secret formula, and it's impossible to anticipate all the problems you might encounter. We spent some time in our weekly staff meeting discussing the session Stewart had with his writer, trying to figure out the best ways to deal with a student whose approach or tone we don't agree with. It helps to have a group discuss these situations, because we're able to try out different perspectives and draw on our various experiences as we come up with possible solutions. But Angela is also right that sensitivity, flexibility, and an open mind will make these sessions productive and maybe even enjoyable.

RECOMMENDED READINGS

THE WRITING PROCESS AND THE TEACHING OF WRITING

Harris, Muriel. "Individualized Diagnosis: Searching for Causes, Not Symptoms of Writing Deficiencies." *College English* 40 (1978): 318–23.

Hartwell, Patrick. "Grammar, Grammars, and the Teaching of Grammar." *College English* 47 (1985): 105–27.

Murray, Donald M. "The Listening Eye: Reflections on the Writing Conference." *College English* 41 (1979): 13–18.

Nystrand, Martin, Stuart Greene, and Jeffrey Wiemelt. "Where Did Composition Studies Come From? An Intellectual History." *Written Communication* 10 (1993): 267–333.

Rose, Mike. "Remedial Writing Courses: A Critique and a Proposal." *College English* 45 (1983): 109–28.

TUTORING IN WRITING CENTERS

Boquet, Elizabeth H. "'Our Little Secret': A History of Writing Centers, Pre- to Post-Open Admissions." *College Composition and Communication* 50 (1999): 463–82.

Brown, John Seely, Allan Collins, and Paul Duguid. "Situated Cognition and the Culture of Learning." *Educational Researcher* 18 (1989): 32–42.

Bruffee, Kenneth A. "Collaborative Learning and the 'Conversation of Mankind.'" *College English* 46 (1984): 635–52.

Carino, Peter. "Early Writing Centers: Toward a History." *The Writing Center Journal* 15 (1995): 103–15.

Ede, Lisa. "Writing as a Social Process: A Theoretical Foundation for Writing Centers?" *The Writing Center Journal* 9 (1989): 3–13.

Harris, Muriel. "Collaboration Is Not Collaboration Is Not Collaboration: Writing Center Tutorials vs. Peer-Response Groups." *College Composition and Communication* 43 (1992): 369–383.

Hobson, Eric H. "Maintaining Our Balance: Walking the Tightrope of Competing Epistemologies." *The Writing Center Journal* 13 (1992): 65–75.

Joyner, Michael A. "The Writing Center Conference and the Textuality of Power." *The Writing Center Journal* 12 (1991): 80–89.

Kail, Harvey. "Collaborative Learning in Context: The Problem with Peer Tutoring." *College English* 45 (1983): 594–99.

Lundsford, Andrea. "Collaboration, Control, and the Idea of a Writing Center." *The Writing Center Journal* 12 (1991): 3–10.

Morrison, Margaret. "Peer Tutors as Postmodern Readers in a Writing Center." *Freshman English News* 18 (1990): 12–15.

North, Stephen M. "Revisiting 'The Idea of a Writing Center'" *The Writing Center Journal* 15 (1994): 7–18.

Trimbur, John. "Literacy Networks: Toward Cultural Studies of Writing and Tutoring." *The Writing Center Journal* 12 (1992): 174–79.

———. "Peer Tutoring: A Contradiction in Terms?" *The Writing Center Journal* 7 (1987): 21–28.

TUTORING ESL STUDENTS

Harris, Muriel, and Katherine E. Rowan. "Explaining Grammatical Concepts." *Journal of Basic Writing* 8 (1989): 21–41.

Harris, Muriel, and Tony Silva. "Tutoring ESL Students: Issues and Options." *College Composition and Communication* 44 (1993): 525–37.

Leki, Ilona. *Understanding ESL Writers.* Portsmouth, NH: Boynton/Cook, 1992.

PRIMARY RESEARCH IN WRITING CENTERS

Bell, James H. *Tutoring in a Writing Center.* Diss. U Texas at Austin, 1989. Ann Arbor: UMI, 1990. 9005528.

Cook-Gumperz, Jenny. "Dilemmas of Identity: Oral and Written Literacies in the Making of a Basic Writing Student." *Anthropology and Education Quarterly* 24 (1993): 336–356.

Davis, Kevin M., Nancy Hayward, Kathleen R. Hunter, and David L. Wallace. "The Function of Talk in the Writing Conference: A Study of Tutorial Conversation." *The Writing Center Journal* 9 (1986): 45–51.

DiPardo, Anne L. "'Whispers of Coming and Going': Lessons from Fannie." *The Writing Center Journal* 12 (1992): 125–144.

Hemmeter, Tom, and Carolyn Mee. "The Writing Center as Ethnographic Space." *The Writing Lab Newsletter* 18 (1993): 4–5.

Lerner, Neal. *Teaching and Learning in a University Writing Center.* Diss. Boston U School of Education, 1996. Ann Arbor: UMI, 1997. 9622601.

MacDonald, Ross B. "An Analysis of Verbal Interactions in College Tutorials." *Journal of Developmental Education* 15 (1991): 2–4, 6, 8, 10, 12.

Magnatto, Joyce Neff. *The Construction of College Writing in a Cross-Disciplinary, Community College Writing Center: An Analysis of Student, Tutor, and Faculty Representations.* Diss. U of Penn., 1991. Ann Arbor: UMI, 1994. 9200369.

Melnick, Jane F. "The Politics of Writing Conferences: Describing Authority Through Speech Act Theory." *The Writing Center Journal* 4 (1984): 9–21.

Roswell, Barbara Sherr. *The Tutor's Audience Is Always a Fiction: The Construction of Authority in Writing Center Conferences.* Diss. U of Penn., 1992. Ann Arbor: UMI, 1994. 9308651.

Severino, Carol. "Rhetorically Analyzing Collaboration(s)." *The Writing Center Journal* 13 (1992): 53–64.

Wolcott, Willa. "Talking It Over: A Qualitative Study of Writing Center Conferencing." *The Writing Center Journal* 9 (1989): 15–29.

Walker, Carol P., and David Elias. "Writing Conference Talk: Factors Associated with High- and Low-Rated Writing Conferences." *Research in the Teaching of English* 21 (1987): 266–285.

LIST OF WORKS CITED

CHAPTER 1: WHY WE TUTOR

Harris, Muriel. "Talking in the Middle: Why Writers Need Writing Tutors." *College English* 57 (1995): 27–42.

CHAPTER 2: THE WRITING PROCESS

Beach, Richard. "Self-Evaluation Strategies of Extensive Rivers and Nonrevisers." *College Composition and Communication* 27 (1976): 160–64.

Berlin, James A. *Rhetoric and Reality: Writing Instruction in American Colleges, 1900–1985.* Carbondale, IL: SIUP, 1987.

Brannon, Lil, and C. H. Knoblauch, "On Students' Rights to Their Own Texts: A Model of Teacher Response." *College Composition and Communication* 33 (1982): 157–66.

Britton, James, Tony Burgess, Nancy Martin, Alex McLeod, and Harold Rosen. *The Development of Writing Abilities (11–18).* London: Macmillan, 1975.

Duncan, C. S. "A Rebellious Word on English Composition." *English Journal* 3 (1914): 154–160.

Elbow, Peter. *Writing Without Teachers.* New York: Oxford UP, 1973.

Emig, Janet. *The Composing Processes of Twelfth Graders.* Urbana, IL: NCTE, 1971.

Faigley, Lester, and Stephen Witte. "Analyzing Revision." *College Composition and Communication* 32 (1981): 400–414.

Flower, Linda, and John A. Hayes. "A Cognitive Process Theory of Writing." *College Composition and Communication* 32 (1981): 365–387.

Flower, Linda, John R. Hayes, Linda Carey, Karen Schriver, and James Stratman. "Detection, Diagnosis and the Strategies of Revision." *College Composition and Communication* 37 (1986): 16–55.

Freire, Paolo. *Pedagogy of the Oppressed.* New York: Herder & Herder, 1972.

Genung, John Franklin. "English at Amherst." *English in the American Universities, by Professors in the English Departments of Twenty Representative Institutions* (1895). Ed. William Morton Payne. In *The Origins of Composition Studies in the American College, 1875–1925.* Ed. John C. Brereton. Pittsburgh: U of Pittsburgh Press, 1995. 172–77.

Grimm, Nancy M. "The Regulatory Role of the Writing Center: Coming to Terms with a Loss of Innocence." *The Writing Center Journal* 17 (1996): 5–29.

Hairston, Maxine. "The Winds of Change: Thomas Kuhn and the Revolution in the Teaching of Writing." *College Composition and Communication* 33 (1982): 76–88.

Lunsford, Andrea. "Collaboration, Control, and the Idea of a Writing Center." *The Writing Center Journal* 12 (1991): 3–10.

Macrorie, Ken. *Telling Writing.* Rochelle Park, NJ: Hayden, 1968.

Murray, Donald M. "The Listening Eye: Reflections on the Writing Conference." *College English* 41 (1979): 13–18.

Paris, Scott G., Margerie Y. Lipson, and Karen K. Wixson. "Becoming a Strategic Reader." *Contemporary Educational Psychology* 8 (1983): 293–316.

Perl, Sondra. "Understanding Composing." *The Writing Teacher's Sourcebook* . Ed. Gary Tate, Edward P. J. Corbett, and Nancy Myers. New York: Oxford UP, 1981. 150–51.

Reigstad, Thomas J., and Donald A. McAndrew. *Training Tutors for Writing Conferences.* Urbana, IL: NCTE, 1984.

Rico, Gabriel L. *Writing the Natural Way.* Los Angeles: J. P. Tarcher, 1983.

Sommers, Nancy. "Revision Strategies of Student Writers and Experienced Adult Writers." *College Composition and Communication* 31 (1980): 378–88.

CHAPTER 3: THE TUTORING PROCESS

Bartholomae, David. "The Study of Error." *College Composition and Communication* 31 (1980): 253–69.

Elbow, Peter, and Pat Belanoff. *A Community of Writers.* New York: Random House, 1989.

North, Stephen M. "The Idea of a Writing Center." *College English* 46 (1984): 433–46.

Reigstad, Thomas J., and Donald A. McAndrew. *Training Tutors for Writing Conferences.* Urbana, IL: NCTE, 1984.

Shaughnessy, Mina P. *Errors and Expectations: A Guide for the Teacher of Basic Writing.* New York: Oxford UP, 1977.

CHAPTER 4: EXAMINING EXPECTATIONS

Barnet, Sylvan and Hugo Bedau. *Critical Thinking, Reading, and Writing: a Brief Guide to Argument, 2nd Ed.* Boston: Bedford, 1996.

Gee, James Paul, Sarah Michaels, and Mary Catherine O'Connor. "The Multifaceted Nature of Discourse Analysis." *The Handbook of Qualitative Research in Education.* Ed. M. D. LeCompte, W. L. Milory, and Judith Preissle. Orlando, FL: Academic Press, 1992. 228–291.

Lunsford, Andrea. "Collaboration, Control, and the Idea of a Writing Center." *The Writing Center Journal* 12 (1991): 3–10.

Mittendorf, Janet G. "Effective Writing Tutors/Advanced Training." Internet. Wcenter, listproc@listserv.acs.ttu.edu (March 8, 1996).

North, Stephen M. "The Idea of a Writing Center." *College English* 46 (1984): 433–46.

Tannen, Deborah. "What's in a Frame? Surface Evidence for Underlying Expectations." *Framing in Discourse*. Ed. Deborah Tannen. New York: Oxford UP, 1993. 14–56.

CHAPTER 7: TAKING NOTES

Barnet, Sylvan and Hugo Bedau. *Critical Thinking, Reading, and Writing: a Brief Guide to Argument*, 2nd Ed. Boston: Bedford, 1996.

CHAPTER 9: READING IN THE WRITING CENTER

Behrens, Laurence, and Leonard J. Rosen. *Writing and Reading Across the Curriculum*, 6th ed. New York: Harper Collins, 1997.

Cole, Michael, and Peg Griffin. "A Sociohistorical Approach to Remediation." *Literacy, Society and Schooling*. Ed. S. deCastell, A. Luke, and K. Egan. Cambridge: Cambridge UP, 1986. 110–131.

Garner, Ruth. *Metacognition and Reading Comprehension*. Norwood, NJ: Ablex, 1986.

Paris, Scott G., Margerie Y. Lipson and Karen K. Wixson. "Becoming a Strategic Reader." *Contemporary Educational Psychology* 8 (1983): 293–316.

Tierney, Robert, and Timothy Shanahan. "Research on the Reading-Writing Relationship: Interactions, Transactions, and Outcomes." *Handbook of Reading Research, Vol. II*. Ed. Rebecca Barr, Michael L. Kamil, Peter Mosenthal, and R. David Pearson. New York: Longman, 1991. 246–80.

Vacca, Richard T., and JoAnne L. Vacca. *Content Area Reading*, 2nd ed. Boston: Little, Brown & Co., 1986.

CHAPTER 10: WORKING WITH ESL WRITERS

Kaplan, Robert. "Cultural Thought Patterns in Inter-Cultural Education." *Language Learning* 16 (1976): 1–20.

Rose, Mike. "Remedial Writing Courses: A Critique and a Proposal." *College English* 45 (1983): 109–28.

CHAPTER 11: DISCOURSE ANALYSIS

Cazden, Courtney B. *Classroom Discourse: The Language of Teaching and Learning*. Portsmouth, NH: Heinemann, 1988.

Davis, Kevin M., Nancy Hayward, Kathleen R. Hunter, and David L. Wallace. "The Function of Talk in the Writing Conference: A Study of Tutorial Conversation." *The Writing Center Journal* 9 (1986): 45–51.

Farb, Peter. *Word Play: What Happens When People Talk.* New York: Bantam, 1973.

Flynn, Thomas. "Promoting Higher-Order Thinking Skills in Writing Conferences." *Dynamics of the Writing Conference: Social and Cognitive Interaction.* Ed. Thomas Flynn and Mary King. Urbana, IL: NCTE, 1993, 3–14.

Hymes, Dell. "Models of the Interaction of Language and Social Life." *Directions in Sociolinguistics: The Ethnography of Communication.* Ed. John J. Gumperz and Dell Hymes. Oxford: Basil Blackwell, 1986. 35–71.

MacDonald, Ross B. "An Analysis of Verbal Interactions in College Tutorials." *Journal of Developmental Education* 15 (1991): 2–4, 6, 8, 10, 12.

Mehan, Harold. *Learning Lessons: Social Organization in the Classroom.* Cambridge, MA: Harvard UP, 1979.

Walker, Carol P., and David Elias. "Writing Conference Talk: Factors Associated with High- and Low-Rated Writing Conferences." *Research in the Teaching of English* 21 (1987): 266–285.

CHAPTER 12: ON-LINE TUTORING

Coogan, Dave. "E-Mail Tutoring: A New Way to Do New Work." *Computers and Composition* 12 (2) (1995): 171–181.

Smith, Erin. "'Here are a few suggestions…': Reading and Readership in the Online Writing Center Conference." Paper presented at Midwest Writing Centers Association Conference, October 23, 1998.

CHAPTER 13: WRITING CENTER ETHICS

Sloan, Jay D. "Ethical Issues." National Writing Centers Association Tutor Stories. Internet. WWW: *http://departments.colgate.edu/diw/NWCAStories.html* (February 1999).

Undergraduate Writing Center, University of Texas at Austin. "Philosophy and Statement of Purpose." Internet. www: http://uwc.fac.utexas.edu/about/uwc_mission.html (November 1, 1998).

INDEX